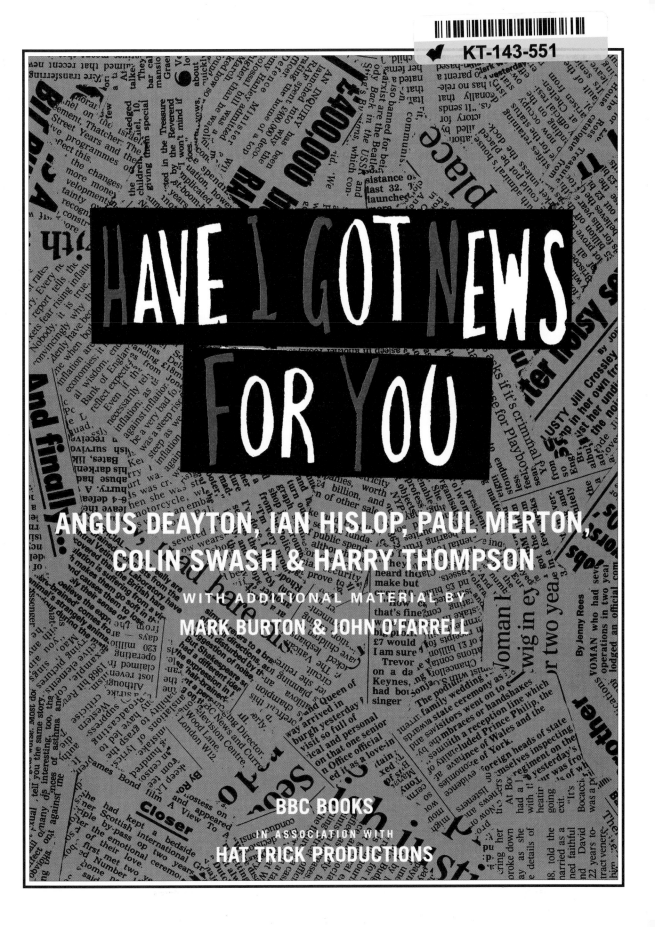

HAVE I GOT NEWS FOR YOU

ANGUS DEAYTON, IAN HISLOP, PAUL MERTON, COLIN SWASH & HARRY THOMPSON

WITH ADDITIONAL MATERIAL BY

MARK BURTON & JOHN O'FARRELL

BBC BOOKS

IN ASSOCIATION WITH

HAT TRICK PRODUCTIONS

Published by BBC Books
a division of BBC Enterprises Limited
Woodlands, 80 Wood Lane,
London W12 0TT

First published 1994

© Hat Trick Productions Ltd. 1994
Design and typesetting © BBC

Title music *Have I Got News For You* © Big George

ISBN: 0 563 37111 0

Designed by Hammond Hammond
Special photography by Tony Lynn-Hill

Printed and bound in Great Britain by BPC Paulton Books Limited
Colour separation by Goodfellow & Egan Limited, Cambridge
Cover printed by Clays Limited, St Ives plc

PICTURE CREDITS

BBC Books would like to thank the following for providing photographs and for permission to
reproduce copyright material. While every effort has been made to trace and acknowledge all
copyright holders, we would like to apologise should there have been any errors or omissions.

All Action Page 33 (top left), 112; Alpha 28 (tl), 57 (bottom); Anglian Press Agency 103 (tl); Ardea
113; Associated Press 11, 43, 55; Courtesy of Austin Reed 80; Roger Bamber 103 (b); Barnaby's 23, 41
(cr), 119 (t), 121 (tr); BBC 58 (b); Biophoto 84 (br); Bournemouth News and Pictures 107; Roland
Boyes 15 (tr); Channel 4 TV 9 (tl); Steve Cox 26 (br); Dennis Print and Publishing 86 (br); Srdja
Djukanovic 14 (t); Monika Duscher 30; Express Newspaper 33 (tr), 97, 127 (tr); © 1994 Hanna-
Barbera Productions Inc. All Rights Reserved 28 (br); Robert Harding 25 (t); Hulton Deutsch
Collection 12, 15 (tl), 18 (br), 32 (b), 90 (t), 108 (bl), 114 (tl) & (br), 124 (tr); Independent Newspaper
81 (centre), 127 (b); Mike Jones 63; Chris Kutschera 117 (tr); Maxwell's Photo Agency 46 (tr);
National Pictures 119 (b); Natural History Museum 108 (br); People Newspaper 79 (b); Andy Phillips
122 (l); Popperfoto 14 (b), 27, 102; Michael Powell 59 (tr); Press Association 8 (tl, bl, br) 16 (bl), 18
(tl), 20, 21, 31, 32 (t), 33 (b), 36, 42, 44, 45 (b), 46 (tl & bl), 52 (t & bl), 57 (t), 59 (b), 60, 62, 66 (t),
68, 76, 81 (t & b), 84 (t & bl), 85 (tr), 90 (br), 91 (r), 93 (t), 98 (b), 100 (b), 108 (tr), 114 (tr), 116 (t),
117 (l), 121 (tl), 122 (r), 124 (tl & br), 127 (tl); Nic Randall 114 (bl); Rex Features 8 (tr), 9 (r), 13, 17
(tl & b), 18 (tr), 28 (t & bl), 37 (tr), 45 (tr), 49 (t), 52 (br), 59 (tl), 63 (bl), 66 (b), 78 (b), 86 (bl), 90
(bl), 103 (tr), 113 (c), 120 (t), 121 (b), 123 (b), 124 (bl), 128; Eric Roberts 57 (c), 87 (t); John
Robertson 15 (b), 54; Solo Syndication 79 (t), 126 (b); Frank Spooner Pictures 17 (tr), 72 (b), 73 (b),
92 (t), 126 (t); Sporting Pictures 18 (bl); Survival Anglia 108 (tl); Syndication International 72 (t), 100
(t); © The Telegraph PLC London, 1993 73 (t), 93 (b); Times Newspapers 58 (t), 75, 78, 87 (b), 92
(b), 95, 106, 116 (b), 117 (br); United Nations Photo 49 (b); Universal Pictorial Press 16 (t), 26 (t), 46
(br); Yorkshire Press Agency 45 (tl); Zefa 40 (b), 41.

Illustrations by Paul Mitchell, Adam Willis, Kevin O'Keefe, Tim Searle, Chris West, Hussein Hussein,
Simon Roulstone, Russell Jones, Helena Zakrzenska-Rucinska.

Front cover photo © BBC; Back cover photo © BBC/Tony Lynn-Hill

ANGUS' *introduction*

Viewers of *Have I Got News For You* will know that it's traditional for me to begin the show with some opening remarks which singularly fail to elicit any response from the audience. These range from 'Hello and welcome to the show that has more column inches than Warren Beatty', to 'Hello and welcome to the show that's done for Friday and Saturday nights what ten pints of lager does for Sunday mornings'; to my own personal favourite, 'Hello and welcome to the show in which we boldly empty the nose of news into the handkerchief of satire'.

So, being a stickler for old values, let me abide by that tradition by saying, 'Hello and welcome to this book, which I think you'll find, when it comes to quality, stops at nothing.'

See?

PAUL'S *introduction*

THE PRODUCERS – A TRIBUTE

Harry Thompson and Colin Swash are two of the dullest individuals currently working in Light Entertainment. Before he broke into television, Harry spent many years paddling around the backwaters of BBC radio producing non-award winning series such as *Cyril Fletcher's Sound Guide to the Colours of the Rainbow*. His pastimes include taking all the credit for *Have I Got News For You* and writing dull books. Two of his efforts, *The Man Behind The Iron Mask* and *Tintin – The Inside Story*, have recently been reprinted in a single volume entitled *Who Cares?*

Colin Swash also comes from radio. His marked sensitivity to acoustics owes much to his former job at Cheam Abattoir. Unlike Harry he has a normal ego and when he first joined *Have I Got News For You* this helped him form a realistic view of his own worth to the programme. This realistic view has led to fifteen suicide attempts – six of which have been successful.

I am thrilled to have this opportunity to publicly salute Harry and Colin's contribution and I am sure I can speak for Angus, Ian and myself when I say, 'Thank you for working on *my* show.'

IAN'S *introduction*

Hello, I'm Ian Hislop. You must be the reader. How do you do?

BEHIND THE SCENES AT

A TYPICAL DAY IN THE LIFE OF BRITAIN'S MOST SUCCESSFUL QUIZ SHOW*

5.00 am The sun rises on a beautiful morning. The day has begun. But not, obviously, for the *Have I Got News For You* team who, as they work in television, won't be getting up for another five-and-a-half hours. Makes you sick, doesn't it?

9.30 am A minicab sets out to fetch Angus Deayton from his London home, to bring him to the studios.

10.30 am The minicab arrives at Khalim's Pork Pie Factory, Dalston E8, having gone to the wrong address for the eleventh week running. Angus boards the number 73 bus.

11.00 am The production team stumble in from their houses, flats, bedsits and police cells. Once assembled, the team gathers around the television set to catch up with all the latest developments on MTV.

11.30 am During a particularly evocative video of 'Jeremy' by Pearl Jam, the boy who delivers the sandwiches happens to mention in passing that the President of the USA has died.

11.33 am Once the video of 'Jeremy' is over, the TV is switched straight to BBC 1, where Anne and Nick's normal programming has been suspended for a special discussion on the implications of the President's death for world affairs, between Clare Rayner, Christopher Biggins and Michaela Strachan.

12.00 noon Ian Hislop arrives at the studio and begins to work through the week's newspapers for stories which may come up in the show. He starts with the *Sunday Times*.

12.30 pm The BBC lawyer, Jane Twitt, arrives with a number of vital points about the week's questions that need clarifying. Can we really get away with calling Ken Livingstone a socialist? Is it really fair to refer to Pol Pot as a mass murderer? What will Mrs Pot say? Can we be sure Liz Taylor has ever been divorced? She is given ten years of old newspapers and told to start at the beginning.

1.00 pm After a tough morning's work, the team repair to a local bar. The production team from *Songs of Praise* are at the next table, from where they throw beer bottles and shout, 'Come and have a go if you think you're hard enough.'

*Well, most successful apart from *A Question of Sport*. And *Family Fortunes*. Oh, and *Bob's Full House*. And *Countdown* of course. Not forgetting *Telly Addicts*, obviously. OK then, it's Britain's least successful quiz show. Apart from Danny Baker's *Pets Win Prizes*.

1.30 pm A confused Angus Deayton arrives at the deserted studios, clutching a bag of pork pies.

1.35 pm A dogged Ian Hislop has worked his way through to the *Sunday Times* 'News Review' section.

1.40 pm Angus nips into make-up for a quick wash and brush up.

6.20 pm Production team return from pub (apart from the runner, who is still looking for his ear after being jumped by three of the *Songs of Praise* team in the gents).

6.30 pm Production team forcibly drag Angus from make-up.

6.45 pm Jack Dee arrives, smiling and laughing as usual.

7.00 pm Roy Hattersley arrives. He is late. He was booked to appear last week.

7.20 pm The show is about to begin and Ian Hislop has to stop reading the week's papers. A pity, as he is still only halfway through the *Sunday Times* 'Style and Travel' section.

7.25 pm Paul Merton arrives at the studio and discreetly slips high-flying researcher Roger Beasley his usual fiver in return for the correct answers.

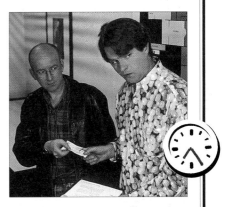

7.29 pm After a panic call from BBC management, all references to Ken Livingstone, Pol Pot and Liz Taylor are removed from the show, on legal advice. Together with any references to Stephen Milligan, who was a friend of John Birt's. Allegedly.

7.30 pm The show begins. Up in the studio gallery, the atmosphere is electric, as the new Madonna video is premiered on MTV.

7.31 pm Ian Hislop abandons all hope of victory.

JEFFREY ARCHER'S
Believe It or Not!

❶ Jeffrey claimed that his 'Simple Truth' concert for the Kurds raised over fifty-seven million pounds whereas the simple truth was that it only raised four million pounds!

❸ Jeffrey was a member of the DCM league, which you can only join if you, or a close relative, hold the Distinguished Conduct Medal. When asked if the William Archer who had won the medal in 1914 was his father, Jeffrey replied, 'I rarely talk about my father and his DCM.' Maybe that's because his father didn't win the DCM – it was a completely different William Archer!

❷ Jeffrey Archer occasionally has a little trouble with his maths. Some years ago, he had to return money to the UN Association – a charitable body – after no fewer than sixty-nine of his expense claims proved to be false!

❹ Jeffrey joined the Metropolitan Police force in 1960. But in the mid-eighties, he denied to *The Times* Diary that he had once been a policeman!

Jeffrey Archer is 'probably the greatest storyteller of our age', according to the *Mail on Sunday*. But did you know he also writes novels?

And did you know…

5 Jeffrey's father was the British Consul in Singapore, according to an interview in the *Guardian* in 1973. The trouble is, Singapore has never had a consul! Jeffrey's father was a local journalist in Weston-Super-Mare!

7 Jeffrey apparently has a qualification from Berkeley University in California. But, mysteriously, when we rang them up, they had no record of him at all!

6 Jeffrey once wrote in the *Sunday Times*, 'Mother was very proud when I got to Oxford. She was very upset when I left after graduating.' Curious, because Jeffrey doesn't have a degree, or any 'A' Levels!

8 When Jeffrey visited Kurdistan, he urged the locals to chant *Bijou Kurdistan*, which he thought meant 'Long live Kurdistan'. In fact *Bijou* means 'Bastard'!

BIJOU JEFFREY ARCHER!

ODD ONE OUT

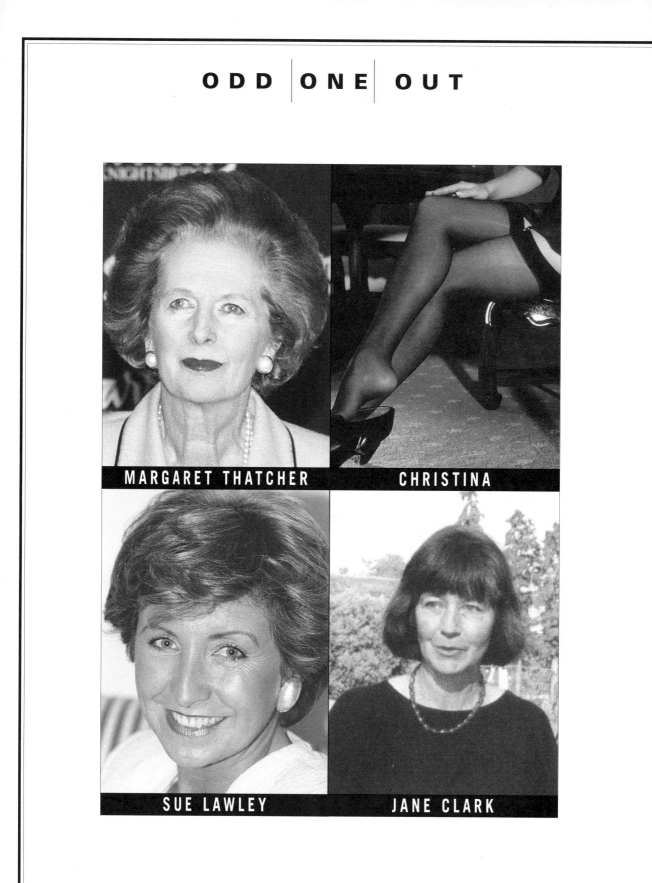

MARGARET THATCHER

CHRISTINA

SUE LAWLEY

JANE CLARK

It's a bit unfair. There's just a pair of legs there called Christina. It could be anyone – Cindy Crawford, Princess Di ... It could have been you Frank, at one time.

Just a small libel, but I'll let it pass.

Can't I do a big one?

The odd one out is Sue Lawley, as according to Alan Clark's diaries, she's the only one the self-confessed lech didn't fancy. The diaries are full of entries such as 'Yesterday, I travelled by train and a plump young lady came into my compartment. She was not wearing a bra and her delightful globes bounced prominently but happily'. The film rights to the diaries have already been bought by Michael Winner.

Clark was even accompanied by an ex-girl-friend, the mysterious Christina, on honeymoon with his wife Jane. He says that other ministers, such as David Mellor, who have had to resign over extra-marital affairs, 'just handled it badly'. He added, 'Mellor got off on the wrong foot.' Yes, it was one of Antonia de Sancha's.

Alan Clark always returns to his wife after his affairs. He wrote, 'I long for darling little Jane, who is always so game and jolly.' Would this be the same 'darling little Jane' that once threw an axe at him?

Clark even found Mrs Thatcher attractive. He wrote, 'I never came across any other woman in politics as sexually attractive in terms of eyes, wrists and ankles.' So, globes not up to scratch then?

My reading of libel is that it has to be untrue, Frank, doesn't it?

. . . .

Still, I'm no expert in the field.

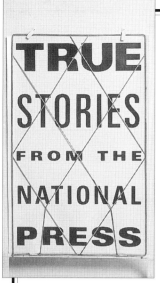

TRUE STORIES FROM THE NATIONAL PRESS

Gasman Ron of Reading to be king

Kampala

FORMER Reading gasman, Ron Mutebi, is to be crowned king of an African state.

He will rule over three million subjects, live in a palace in Kampala, and be listed in Yellow Pages under 'Kings'.

Ron has been told to take up his throne immediately – so he'll be round in about six months, although he can't say whether it'll be morning or afternoon.

He's already confident that he could handle a constitutional crisis. 'Oh, that'll be your upper chamber impeding the parliamentary process, mate. You'll need a pink form from Basingstoke.'

When Prince Charles heard the story, he was impressed by the notion of a man exchanging a meaningless life for a truly worthwhile existence. And immediately applied for Ron's old job at the gas board.

Keep dying, you're on video

New York

When her husband Robert had a heart attack, New York housewife Rose Langdon dived for the video camera and recorded it in the hope that it would be shown on a Jeremy Beadle-style show.

Presumably a show in which viewers have to vote on which is the funniest near-fatal incident, and the winner gets a 'You've Been Filmed Dying' t-shirt.

Mr Langdon later said that he wouldn't have minded, but it was when she stopped to touch up his make-up that he got really annoyed.

Instant sunshine in the politburo

Berlin

Those merciless sadists, the Politburo, have admitted that they used to instruct East German weathermen to issue completely bogus forecasts of warm and sunny weather for every official occasion.

After five years of eighty-two-degree forecasts for the New Year's Day Parade in East Berlin, it's surprising that nobody smelt a rat. Probably because they had already roasted it for Christmas dinner.

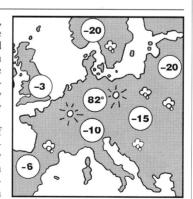

Official Weather Forecast. Christmas Day, Berlin.

OXFORD KEEPS OVERSEAS STUDENTS IN LINE

Brussels

European education authorities have reacted angrily to a plan that has been drawn up to teach foreign students at Oxford the English art of queueing.

Students will also be taught that when someone else pushes in, the correct procedure is to tut quietly and whisper 'honestly'.

Apparently local residents in Oxford don't like foreign students pushing in at the front of the queue. Actually they don't like them standing at the back of the queue either. Basically, they just don't like them.

The initiative has won support from the Polite Society, set up in 1987 to encourage a more courteous Britain. A spokesman for the society said, 'It will hopefully bring about some sense of decorum and consideration for others in these stroppy foreign gits.'

For the sake of balance, Oxford authorities said they would like to make it clear that there are a large number of foreign students who don't push in front of people at the checkout. They're too busy shoplifting.

Bleak thrills at Stasiworld

Berlin

Stasiworld, a new theme park, has been set up north of Berlin and promises all visitors an authentic East German experience.

The only cars for hire will be Trabants, most of the shops will be empty, meals will be eaten with aluminium cutlery, you'll come second in the Olympics and your country's economic system will grind to a halt and merge with a western market economy.

It'll be just five pounds to get in, and twenty-five pounds to get out.

Owner Frank Georgi said it would be a chance for ordinary East Germans to find out what the 'Stasi' secret police were really like. As it seems that most East Germans use to work for the Stasi, they should know already.

Radio girl's tot will be air-born

Canberra

Radio DJ Suki Mead, of Australia's CFM, has decided to give birth live on air. She admits it could be difficult to keep up the DJ patter in such circumstances. As the baby comes out, she could find herself saying, 'And joining me now in the studio ....' or, 'Stay tuned – we'll be back after my waters break.'

The idea comes from a US radio sports journalist who had a vasectomy while reading his column on air (so to speak).

Experts are now wondering where it'll end – Simon Bates having a frontal lobotomy live on air? Would anyone notice?

REGGAE FAN STRUNG UP

Florida

Rastafarian Zachary Brown has appeared in court in Monroe County, Florida, charged with playing reggae music too loudly in public.

Judge Wayne Miller sentenced him to spend two hours a day, for thirty days, in a lift at the county library, listening to 'Easy Listening Music' by the 101 Strings Orchestra. Mr Brown said he would prefer to be sent to Alcatraz for life. As should whoever dreamed up the idea of music in lifts.

The incident demonstrates the difference between judges in America and Britain. In Britain, most judges would consider the 101 Strings Orchestra an example of dangerous, drug-crazed, head-banging rock 'n' roll.

Mr Brown has now been warned that if he re-offends, he'll get sixty days in an airport lounge.

Japanese up to their ears in jewels from the sewers

Tokyo

THE Tokyo Metropolitan Sewerage Bureau have discovered they can make jewellery from human waste, or 'de-watered sludge' as it's known after treatment.

A top Japanese recording artist has already released a hit record, 'De-watered sludge items are a girl's best friend'.

The idea originally came from a bureau worker who was apparently 'struck by the lustre of slag'. Alan Clark says he knows the feeling.

The Japanese say they can also make vases out of the dried human waste, as long as nobody tries adding water.

'Sludge' can be used to make notepaper, business cards and folders as well. Just as long as they don't use it to make stamps.

The uglies are sitting pretty

Santa Cruz

A law was passed yesterday by the Santa Cruz City Council, prohibiting job discrimination against people who are ugly.

The legislation is aimed at protecting those who are 'fat, short, toothless, gormless or just anatomically repulsive'. That should come as a relief to Andrew Lloyd Webber.

The case that provoked it involved a woman who was rejected for a job at a health food shop because she weighed twenty-one stones. But under the new law, she's managed to find herself a job as a chimney sweep – which looks like being a permanent position.

WASHINGTON: There are fears that, as a result of the Whitewater Scandal, Hillary Clinton may have dramatically lost weight.

Ve have vays of making you kip

Vienna

Austrian hotelier, Erwin Wagner, has outraged several English holiday-makers staying at his establishment. One guest even filmed him ripping a door off its hinges and pinning a customer to the wall with it. Herr Wagner has now been offered the lead role in *Terminator 3*.

Herr Wagner also angered guests by closing the hotel bar at nine o'clock on the dot. He said, 'I know the English. They drink gin and whisky when I've gone to bed.' They were probably in bed throwing up, if they were drinking gin with whisky.

Herr Wagner has now complained that the British press have stereotyped him as a World War II cliché. He said it wasn't his fault as he was bound by the law to close the hotel bar at nine o' clock. He told reporters, 'I vos only obeying last orders.'

TV's *Mr Sex*

by our showbiz staff, Tina Blind

Witty, knowledgeable and authoritative he may be, but to millions of female viewers, Angus Deayton is simply TV's Mr Sex. He's the man who opens girls' hearts and sets their legs a-flutter. But just what makes a human being *that* sexy?

The genes of a normal male have one Y chromosome for every X chromosome. Scientists have identified a strain of so-called 'supermales': superior men who have two Y chromosomes for every X. Angus Deayton has forty-seven Y chromosomes. Admittedly that's the total number in his entire body, but he's still pretty damned sexy.

There is not a single chromophore in Angus' body. Chromophores are groups of atoms generally, in an organic compound, that absorb light of characteristic wavelengths. Typical examples are the azo ($-N=N-$) and nitroso ($-N=O$) groups. Auxo-chromes help to modify the colour conferred by the chromophore. A group derived from sulphuric acid ($-SO_3H$) is a typical auxochrome. The chromophore is not actually anything to do with the chromosome, but it is right next to it in the dictionary, so whole passages about it are often copied out by mistake. Still, he's pretty sexy, eh girls?

Angus is but the latest in a long line of holders of the presti-gious TV's Mr Sex title, which has, of course, been running since television began. The first TV's Mr Sex was BBC announcer Corbett Brownlow, who held the title from 1936–1939 (evenings only).

Brownlow: the first-ever TV's Mr Sex.

Angus has now qualified for Europe and in 1991 represented Britain at the bi-annual *Monsieur Sex de Télévision de l'Europe* contest, where he carried off the coveted Golden Globe Award. Police stopped him at the door.

Two years later, the going was even tougher. After an easy first-round win over Vitali Podgorny – popular front-man of Ukrainian television's *Potato Roadshow* – he crashed out in the second round to

THE FULL LIST OF HOLDERS	
1936–1939	Corbett Brownlow
1939–1945	title suspended for duration of hostilities
1945–1951	John Snagge
1951–1954	Peter Glaze
1954–1963	Fanny and Johnny Cradock (joint holders)
1963–1965	Peter Glaze (following hip operation)
1965–1969	Fanny Cradock (WBA version) Johnny Cradock (WBC version) Peter Glaze (WBO version)
1969–1972	Henry Cooper (title re-unified following 5th round KO)
1972–1974	Joe Bugner
1974 (March)	Raymond Baxter
1974–1975	Peter 'Blue Peter' Purves (before 6 pm) Frank 'Frank' Finlay (after 6 pm)
1975–1989	Frank Bough (also 'TV's Mrs Sex' from 1988 onwards).
1990–?	Angus Deayton

Lars Folstrup, steamy host of Norway's top-rated *Tryggve og Haugesund Vesteralen Pørky Pørky Peephøl*.

Angus, as he might look (but doesn't).

What of the future? **H**ow long will Angus remain TV's Mr Sex? **W**ho will replace him? **W**ill lasting peace ever come to the Balkans?

☆ **Answer these questions and you could win a fabulous prize…**

Win a Dream Date with

ANGUS DEAYTON

On your dream date with Angus you will be

Driven by limousine to Old Trafford to watch Manchester United draw 0–0 with Ipswich.

Entertained by Angus' collection of Genesis and early Pink Floyd albums.

Whisked away to a five-star restaurant, and left there, while Angus goes off to record various voice-overs.

Note: This is his dream date, not yours.

NEWS JUST IN

BBC

Looking back on her years in office, Mrs Thatcher unveils her dream cabinet.

There are reports that privatising the London-Southend railway line has failed to ease overcrowding.

In Russia, a historic photograph has been discovered which shows the origin of the mark on Mikhail Gorbachev's head.

After the latest round of BBC cost-cutting, Basil Brush finds out his contract hasn't been renewed.

. . . and the FA opens the new George Best School of Football Excellence.

Martyn Lewis

news

Hello, children. Are you sitting comfortably...? It's the Martyn Lewis News! Your favourite newscaster, who wants to banish all the beastly stories from news bulletins, is here with his latest round-up.

Giant IRA bomb rocks City. 'The best news we've had in ages,' say glaziers.

A triumph for British technology, as the Hawk jet demonstrates its versatility in the massacre of East Timorese civilians.

Britain maintains its noble tradition of backing the underdog by giving continued assistance to Pol Pot, the plucky little leader of the Khmer Rouge.

It's boom-time for undertakers, as it's officially admitted that a total of thirty-four people have been murdered by psychiatric patients released under the Care In The Community scheme.

'We do not support the Khmer Rouge in any way.'

(Douglas Hurd, Foreign Secretary, 1991)

'Her Majesty's Government has provided training to the armed forces of the Cambodian non-communist resistance.'

(Archie Hamilton, Defence Minister, 1991)

'There has been full tactical military cooperation between the non-communist Cambodian forces and Pol Pot's Khmer Rouge.'

(George Bush, 1991)

and finally...

TV newscaster Martyn Lewis is stopped for speeding and banned from driving for six months. Another triumph in the battle against irresponsibility on Britain's roads.

ODD ONE OUT

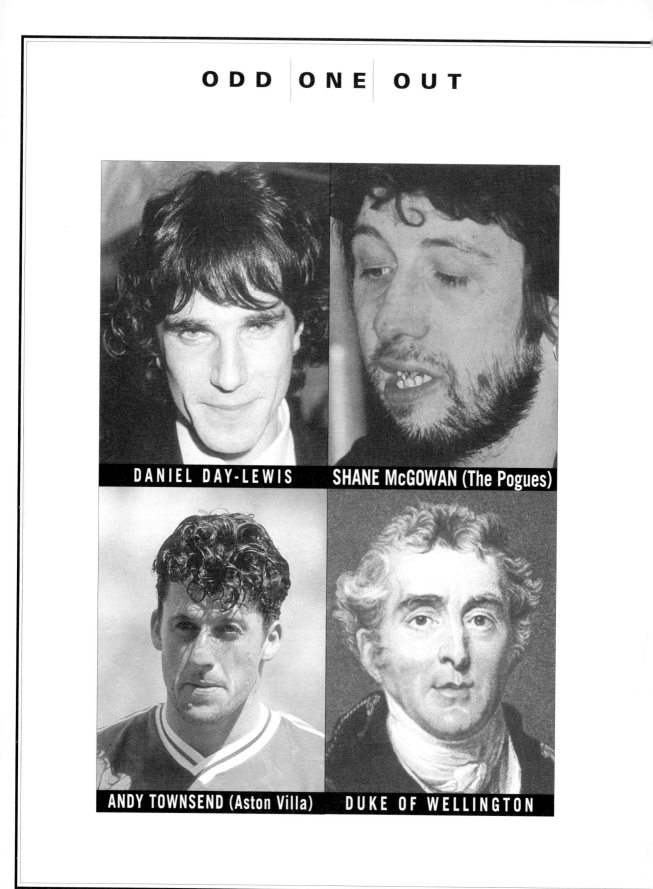

DANIEL DAY-LEWIS

SHANE McGOWAN (The Pogues)

ANDY TOWNSEND (Aston Villa)

DUKE OF WELLINGTON

ANSWERS

What are the Pogues?

A popular beat combo.

Is the Duke of Wellington the odd one out?

He didn't play for Aston Villa, did he?

The odd one out *is* the Duke of Wellington, as the others all act as if they're Irish even though they were born in England. The Duke, on the other hand, preferred to see himself as English although he was born in Ireland. Once, when called an Irishman, Wellington said, 'Being born in a stable does not make one a horse.' No, Jesus would probably be with him on that one.

Shane McGowan was born in England and educated at Westminster Public School, but he claims fifty per cent Irish blood. The other fifty being a mix of vodka, whisky and meths.

Andy Townsend, the Republic of Ireland football captain, was born in Maidstone, Kent, and only got a chance to play in the Ireland team because of his Irish grandmother. She pulled a hamstring just before the Denmark match.

Daniel Day-Lewis was born in London, but became an Irish citizen at the age of thirty. He recently denied that he has started to affect his Irishness, although he *was* wearing a green suit and carrying a pig under his arm at the time.

Hang on a minute! Why should Irish people be carrying a pig under their arm?

It's just a caricature, like Scotsmen wearing kilts.

My mother's Irish, so should I walk around with half a pound of sausages under my arm?

Well, I have an English father and a Scottish mother. Which means I'm both stuck-up and mean.

There are pigs in the West Midlands that have Irishmen under their arms.

THE WoAD TO STARDoM

CONTROVERSIAL film director Ken Russell has devised the novel idea of filming Fergie in the nude, in his new movie about Boadicea. A palace spokesman was outraged at the suggestion, saying there was nothing at all novel about filming Fergie in the nude.

It has subsequently emerged that the Duchess isn't prepared to play the part. Although she *is* prepared to claim to have written the script.

Fergie was concerned at the idea of having to watch armies of unclothed women marching into battle and being whipped naked. Her father, Major Ronald Ferguson, said that, rather than let anybody down, he was more than willing to stand in for her.

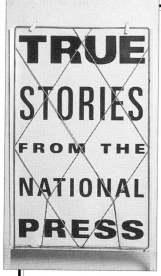

The Royal Family reacts to news that Andrew Morton has been struck by lightning.

WILLIAM'S ROYAL FLUSH

PRINCE WILLIAM, heir to the throne, has been caught pushing a fellow pupil's head down a lavatory at Ludgrove School. It's feared he has been spending too long in Uncle Andrew's company.

The school has decided not to name the victim to save him from embarrassment - although fellow pupils say that he's easy enough to spot.

The headmaster called William in and strongly warned him that if he thought he could get away with that sort of behaviour, he was absolutely right. And could he please have a knighthood.

LAUNDRY BILL OF £63 000

IT'S been revealed that Her Majesty The Queen spends an annual £63 000 on laundry.

Presumably, she uses the service wash.

It's also been announced that Her Majesty spends £2.3 million a year on travel by train. Experts have pointed out that if she'd applied for a railcard she could have cut it down to £1.5 million.

British Rail say they may now introduce a 'Queen Card', where you get an entire liveried carriage to yourself. But only after half past nine.

Princess Diana Bites The Bullet

PRINCESS Diana has spoken in public about anorexia and bulimia. She told a conference of experts on eating disorders, 'If you eat you live, if you don't you die.' The revelation came as something of a shock to them. A spokesman admitted it was the kind of blinding thought that makes the Royal family worth every penny.

The princess referred to the illness as 'a shameful friend that stays with you for life'. As opposed to the sort that rings you up at three in the morning and doesn't say a word.

Diana is apparently now free of the disease, but at one point used to swallow handfuls of laxatives. Which explains why she made such short speeches in those days. Dr Jane Ogden of the Middlesex Hospital said of her speech, 'It was a very brave thing to do.' A cowardly person, for instance, would have attacked her husband in print anonymously, by getting a *Daily Star* journalist to ghost-write a book of her allegations.

SSHH! ONE'S THINKING

ON A VISIT to Charing Cross Station, Princess Anne asked for all the announcements to be switched off for four hours because they were too noisy, thereby causing confusion and delays across the whole Kent region. So, no change there.

The reason given was that she was thinking. Good job it wasn't Princess Di or they would have had to close down the whole of London.

NEWS HAVE WE FOR THEM GOT!

THE ASTONISHINGLY ORIGINAL WORLD OF NEWSPAPER HEADLINE-WRITING

THE FIRST appearance of *Have I Got News For You* on 29 September 1990 was to change the world of headline-writing for ever. Previously, journalists had floundered in their attempts to distil news stories into a single pithy phrase, but scientists now estimate that up to 40 per cent of all Fleet Street headlines are based on the trusty 'Have I Got X for You' formula. Here are some of the more cunning examples:

HAVE I GOT BOOZE FOR YOU Fears for Angus' alcohol consumption in the *Sunday Mirror* when he freely admits to journalists that he consumes as much as a bottle of wine every week. That's almost a glass a day.

HAVE I GOT CASH FOR YOU Shock news in the *Sunday People* that Paul Merton has visited a cash-dispenser – interestingly enough, quite near to his home.

HAVE I GOT HUGHES FOR YOU An amazing discovery in the *Sun* that not only does Angus Deayton support Manchester United, but – joy of joys – the United squad includes a player whose name rhymes with 'news'.

HAVE I GOT KNEES FOR YOU The *Sun* follows up its top 'Hughes' exclusive with the revelation that when Angus plays football, the gap between his socks and his shorts reveals his knees. And – even more satisfyingly – the word 'knees' forms a pleasing half-rhyme with the word 'news'.

HAVE WE GOT VIEWS FOR YOU It's Angus again, as the *Mail on Sunday* announces to a punch-drunk readership that on his forthcoming Himalayan holiday, the chairman of BBC 2's popular news-based quiz will be taking in a number of scenic panoramas.

HAVE THEY GOT VIEWS FOR YOU In a subtle variation, the *Radio Times* reveals that guests who have appeared on the programme have in some cases formed opinions about the experience. To their extreme disappointment, the magazine offers none of them a free holiday in the Himalayas, complete with fawning profile.

HAVE I GOT NEWS FOR YOU The *Times* rather misunderstands the concept, and in a tawdry exposé of the panellists' love lives, completely fails to change even one word of the programme's title.

HAVE I GOT CUES FOR YOU In an amazing showbiz exclusive, the *Daily Express* reveals that the entire programme is scripted from start to finish – which comes as a nasty shock to Ian and Paul, whose tendency to turn up an hour before each recording doesn't leave them much time to memorise half-an-hour's-worth of material.

HAVE I GOT NEWS FOR YOU … I QUIT More blisteringly accurate showbiz gossip from *Today*, who are able to reveal exclusively that Angus will be leaving the show in the autumn of 1993.

HAVE THEY GOT NEWS FOR NEIL Women faint and strong men break down in tears as *Today* newspaper blows the formula wide open, replacing the word 'you' instead of the word 'news'. And the 'news' for Neil Kinnock? Several months ago, he may recall, he agreed to appear on TV's *Have I Got News For You*.

HAVE WE GOT NEW HAVE I GOT NEWS FOR YOU HEADLINES FOR YOU

Despite literally scores of headlines in this vein, the possibilities have not yet been exhausted. Here are some future headlines to look out for:

'HAVE I GOT FLUES FOR YOU' Angus has his chimney swept by a small boy in direct contravention of the Climbing Boys Act of 1840.

'HAVE I GOT SCREWS FOR YOU' Suspicious that his wife may be having an affair, Paul Merton rushes into his bedroom to find the wardrobe door hanging slightly loose at its hinges.

'HAVE I GOT PEWS FOR YOU' Ian Hislop is made Bishop of Launceston.

'HAVE I GOT TROOS FOR YOU' Angus buys a pair of trousers from a traditionally-minded Aberdeen retailer.

'HAVE I GOT LOOS FOR YOU' Shock revelations in the *Sunday Mirror* that the team captains' perks include unrestricted use of studio washroom facilities.

NOTE: To avert any more of this tiresome use of the *Have I Got News For You* title, the producers would like to announce that as of April 1995, the programme will be renamed *Mother Theresa in Gonorrhoea Shock*.

HAVE I GOT CUES FOR YOU!

★ *by our showbiz editor*

Mackay and Lymeswold.

Top BBC 1 quiz *Have I Got News For You* is a total sham.

SO SAY TV scriptwriters Jock Mackay and Arthur Lymeswold. Mackay and Lymeswold make the astonishing claim that they have scripted every single show of the top-rated panel game since it was first broadcast in July 1973.

'Every word you hear, not to mention every cough, sneeze or hesitation, has been scripted by us,' say the two veteran funny-men. 'Every time you see Ian, Paul or Andrew make a joke, you can be sure it's one of ours.'

Mackay and Lymeswold say they start work on each show up to four months ahead of trans-mission, which, as it's a topical programme, usually involves predicting what major world events are liable to happen in the week that the show goes out. 'We were dead chuffed when we second-guessed the assassination of Anwar Sadat,' says sixty-seven-year-old Lymeswold, 'and the collapse of the Warsaw Pact was frankly a lucky guess. Sadly, the Archbishop of Canterbury drug bust was a little embarrassing.'

Have We Got News For You is not the only programme in Mackay and Lymeswold's long list of credits. As well as the Wednesday night quiz, the BBC also uses them to write the commentary for the Wimbledon Men's Singles Final and all Jeremy Paxman's *Newsnight* links. Once in a while they are given the important task of scripting Richard Dimbleby's live *Election Night* specials. 'Interviews with exuberant Liberal-Democrats are our favourite,' says Lymeswold, 'although Charles Kennedy always insists on writing his own ad-libs.'

A spokesman for Hat Rack Productions, who make *Have They Got News For You*, denied all knowledge of Mackay and Lymeswold. He told our reporter, 'I'm sorry, could you speak up? You sound a little drunk.'

*h*ave I Got News For You is now so popular that versions of it are shown in different countries all around the world. Some of them bought our idea, some of them stole our idea, and one of them even thought of it several years before we did. Bastards. Here's how the programme looks across the globe.

· IRAQ ·

عندي لكاخبــار (pronounced '*Andi Lak Akhbar*'), the Middle East's most rebellious satire show, is known for its political contrasts: one team supports Saddam, while the other violently opposes his enemies. Rounds include: Saddam News Film, Saddam Headlines, Odd Saddam Out and Find The Missing Saddam.

· IRELAND ·

Haugh Ai Goiaot Nueoughs Fiorr Youaaigh (pronounced 'Have I Got News For You') is Ireland's most popular panel game for men with pigs under their arm. The only difference from the British version is that the pigs don't wear loud shirts and win every week.

· C H I N A ·

有新闻给你吗 , China's wackiest news quiz, has disappointing viewing figures of just 795 million a week – although the running gag about declining rice harvests in the Jungshau autonomous region brings the house down every time.

· J A P A N ·

To viewers of 何か、ニュース はありますかね, the scale of Ian Hislop's failure in Britain is as nothing compared to the failure of losing captains Ryuchi Ikemori, Yukei Kasahara, Yoshiko Taniguchi, Hiromi Go, Tosaki Sashimi, Kiyotaka Nagasawa. This week's guests are two well-known regulars on Japanese television, Shohei Yamada and Tony Slattery.

· S W E D E N ·

The Swedes pride themselves on providing wholesome family television before the 5.00 pm watershed and *Har Du Hört Det Senaste* is no exception. Chairman Bo Deaytsson is known and admired throughout Scandinavia as TV's Mr Sexless, on account of his unique lack of sex appeal.

can s... Night hunters of... BT slashes
Bring back tour collap...
...tate
...respondent
...train failed to...
Bolshoi

Missing Words

THE QUEEN JOINS ▮

Queen? Now Freddie Mercury's gone.

Everton?

Joins her husband on holiday. Unlike any other member of the Royal Family.

Now that would be news.

ANSWER: E.C. Row

JOYOUS FERGIE MOVES IN WITH ▮

Saddam Hussein?

Finally meeting her match.

That's very unfair on Saddam.

Is it Charlton Heston?

More likely Charlton Athletic.

Large doughnut?

ANSWER: Cast iron bathtub

HOSPITALS TOLD TO CUT COSTS BY USING ▮

No doctors?

Back copies of *Private Eye* as a general anaesthetic.

Anyone watch Paul Merton's programme on Channel 4? Me neither.

Now, now, girls.

ANSWER: Temporary staff

I MADE THATCHER ▮ BOASTS NIGEL.

Is it 'Swallow'?

(Panel incapable of making any further suggestions.)

ANSWER: Act

CAPTION COMPETITION

ODD | ONE | OUT

TREVOR McDONALD

ANNE DIAMOND

JIMMY SAVILE

YOGI BEAR

ANSWERS

> *Just think back, have you been to bed with any of those people?*

> *I'm not answering that.*

> *The one in the white hat? You must remember. You got drunk, you were in Jellystone Park…*

The odd one out is Yogi Bear, as he's the only one never to have been voted 'Tie Man of the Year', which seems particularly harsh as that's the only article of clothing he wears.

Trevor McDonald, who won the award in 1990, has frequently tried to read *News at Ten* Yogi Bear-style, wearing only his tie. ITN bosses have told him if he tries it one more time, it's back to 'Newsroom Grampian'.

Jimmy Savile was voted the most stylish tie-wearer of the 1970s – bit like being voted 'butchest hairdresser'.

And Anne Diamond bizarrely became 'Tie Man of the Year' 1986 – the very same year that the Miss UK title was won by Mike Morris.

> *So that's 'no comment' is it Trevor?*

> *Bong! Trevor McDonald refuses to answer the question.*

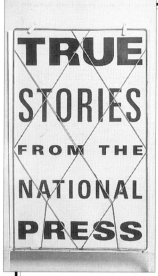

TRUE STORIES FROM THE NATIONAL PRESS

Is the porridge to your satisfaction?

THE prison version of the citizen's charter is a hotel-style questionnaire which has been sent to prisoners all over the country, asking how their conditions can be improved. The most popular requests so far have been for lower walls, thinner bars and the right to receive very long thin cakes from home.

Prisoners were asked whether they preferred to eat inside or outside their cells. The consensus was 'about 300 miles outside'.

They were also asked how they rated their laundry facilities, how they enjoyed their leisure time and how they liked their warders – trussed and stuffed, probably.

Cheep victory

BUDGIE-FANCIER Mr Fred Kennedy of West Yorkshire has won the case brought against him by his next-door neighbours, Mr and Mrs Fussey.

In an effort to prove that Mr Kennedy's budgies were chirping too raucously, the Fusseys hired top Zimbabwean noise expert, Professor Joe McNulty – a genius in all aspects of his field, apart from the fact that he was deaf.

When Gerald Lumley, counsel for Mr Kennedy said, 'I put it to you that you are hard of hearing,' Professor McNulty replied, 'Yes, I am.' Thereby depriving everyone of the joke they were expecting.

Mr Kennedy said, 'There have been problems throughout the time we have lived next door to the Fusseys.' Still, not half as many as with the neighbours on the other side, Mr and Mrs Shagging-on-the-lawn.

For their part, the Fusseys say they've had enough, and they're moving to get away from their awkward neighbours. They've just found a very reasonably priced terraced house in Cromwell Street, Gloucester.

Thief takes a shine to his victim's cars

A SHEFFIELD man who stole people's cars, washed them, polished them, and then brought them back again, has gone on trial at York Magistrates Court.

The thief's name is Colin Sadd. Frankly, is you're called Mr and Mrs Sadd there's not a lot you can do for your son, but calling him 'Colin' is hardly the answer.

Sadd, a car enthusiast who failed to find a job in a garage, courteously returned every car spotlessly clean and in excellent mechanical condition. No wonder he couldn't get a job in a garage.

After being sentenced, Mr Sadd left the court in a police transit van ... which they hope he'll bring back soon.

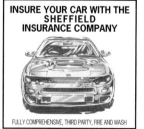
Judge Dread

AT a court in Fort Lauderdale, Florida, Judge J. Leonard Fleet pulled a gun on defendant Gordon Meyette, pointed it at him, and threatened to pull the trigger.

Afterwards he added: 'Whether I put a bullet into the cylinder is for me to know and the defendant to guess.' Although the defendant would have a pretty good guess with half his head blown away.

The judge took this action because Meyette

An embarrassing scene in London's West End as police raid a Soho brothel.

had been waving his arms and making faces at him. Just as well the judge never went into the teaching profession.

Defence lawyer Lawrence Wolk said the judge was just like Clint Eastwood saying, 'Go ahead punk, make my day.' Of course that could never happen here. A British judge would simply bring out a musket and say: 'Proceed young man, to enhance my enjoyment of the forthcoming twenty-four hours.'

The banana bandit who slipped up

SELF-STYLED 'Banana Bandit' Carl Lancaster has been arrested for holding up a Shell petrol station with a cucumber.

Apparently he pointed it at the cashier and said: 'If you don't give me a lot of money I will shoot you.' Whereupon the cashier gave him sixty pounds. Obviously scared of cucumbers.

Instead of making his escape in a getaway car though, Lancaster is said to have hailed a cab, which promptly got stuck in a traffic jam. Nice to know that happens to bank robbers as well, isn't it?

Police later recovered his carrier bag containing a cucumber, a bunch of bananas and a sawn-off aubergine.

Mr Inlandi Revendi nicks £7 000 000 off taxman

A group of Post Office workers has been caught stealing £7 million worth of cheques made out to the Inland Revenue, which they banked in accounts opened under the name of Mr Inlandi Revendi.

So it won't be very long before Mr Revendi gets a visit from Mr Fraudi Squadi.

In one case, a building society accepted an altered cheque for £175 000, but claimed it had taken action to check the identity of the customer. Presumably the procedure went along the lines of, 'This your name?' 'Yup.' 'Fine, here's £175 000.'

He's guilty... it's written all over his ears

POLICE now say that when it comes to catching criminals, the shape of the human ear is as individual as a finger print.

So burglars will have to be very careful, when breaking into someone's house, not to stick their ears into any soft putty they may find.

The science of ear-printing is not new. One researcher has been collecting ear-prints for the last thirty-eight years (that makes train spotting seem almost interesting). Apparently ears are categorised in three sizes. Small, medium and Royal family.

Scientists now claim that it won't be long before they can reconstruct the face of a bank robber just by looking at the tights he was wearing over his head. Always assuming his wife doesn't wear them again before the police get hold of them, or they'll be looking for a man with extremely chubby cheeks or a triangular beard. If Jeremy Beadle is arrested for the Brinks-Mat job, we'll know what's happened.

Prisoner's Chicken Fantasy

BURGLAR Rob Ferguson, imprisoned in Wolds Remand Centre (run by Group 4 Security), has taken so many narcotics that he now believes himself to be a chicken.

Apparently, thirty-year-old Robert had a drugs problem before being taken into prison. But now he has no problem getting drugs at all.

Robert's lawyer, Mr Simon Reevell, said: 'He was given far greater access to drugs in prison than he got on the streets of Scarborough.' Mr Reevell then applied on behalf of his client for the sentence to be tripled.

Group 4 deny that there are any hardened drug dealers in their care, saying that they'd be miles away by now.

ROB FERGUSON ON HIS WAY TO THE COURT OF APPEAL.

Justice is a ferret down the trousers

A VIGILANTE group in Newton, Powys, has announced that any local criminals they catch will be frogmarched to the hills and have a vicious ferret, named Fred, forcibly inserted into their trousers.

Apparently, if Fred sees a juicy thigh he gives it a nasty nip. But if he sees what looks like another ferret the consequences are far, far worse.

Leader of the group David Evans said: 'It will teach any criminal a lesson he won't forget in a hurry.' That's if you can still refer to him as a 'he'.

The group wear masks over their heads so no one knows who they are. It's just the half-dozen ferrets hanging off their belts that give them away. Little balaclavas are now being made for the ferrets to protect *their* identity.

In preparation for his next vigilante film, Michael Winner agreed to have a number of ferrets stuffed down his underpants. The ferrets later had to be brought round with smelling salts.

★ *LAWYERS' NOTE: In no way is the above to be interpreted as a suggestion that Mr Winner's underpant hygiene is anything other than of the most pristine standard. The ferrets merely fainted at what they saw in there.*

With this pistol I thee nick

At an underworld wedding in Corunna, Michigan, the bride turned out to be an undercover police officer, as did the groom, the band and half the congregation.

The unlucky half of the congregation, including the father of the bride, were all drug dealers and were promptly arrested. Apparently it was the only wedding in history where the bride gave the father away.

999 call scandal

British Telecom have been accused of passing 999 calls to police, fire and ambulance services in the wrong areas. Two blazes in Ulster were referred to firemen in North Wales, a fire in Huddersfield was passed to Humberside, a Leicester fire to Derby, and a Worksop fire to Nottingham.

By the time they arrived, the fire had probably spread that far anyway.

We telephoned a British Telecom spokesman for his reaction and he asked us what topping we wanted on our pizza.

A tomato dials 999

Meanwhile, in West Virginia, armed police burst into a house in response to a series of 999 calls, only to find that there was no one there and that they'd been telephoned by a tomato. Apparently it was growing right next to the nine button on the phone.

The phone company admitted they found it bizarre that a tomato should make repeated calls to the police, but it was when it rang the operator to query its bill that they really began to worry.

A spokesman admitted that it was uncommon for a vegetable to telephone the operator. Normally you call the operator and get connected to a vegetable.

NEWS JUST IN

John Major reveals exactly what he's taken out of Scotland.

East End police cells are full after a riot at the Garry Bushell lookalike contest.

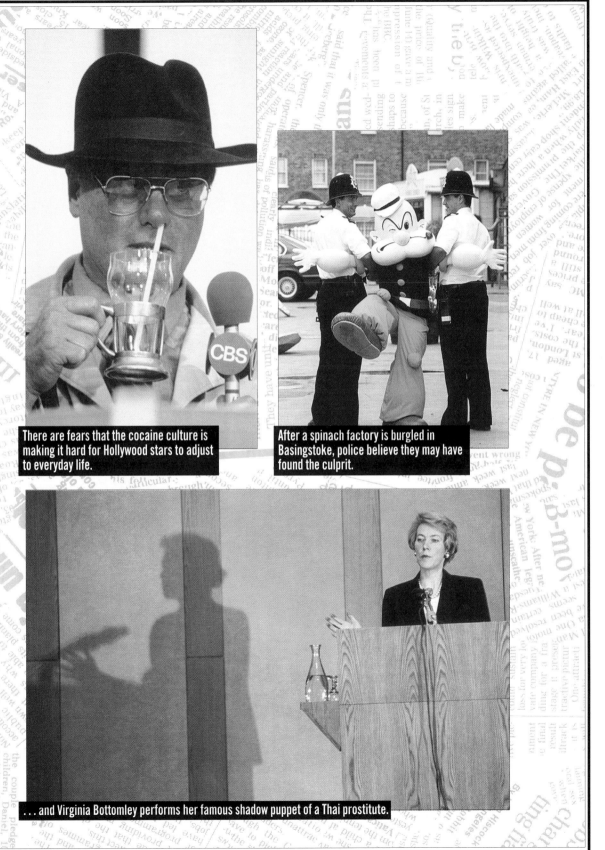

There are fears that the cocaine culture is making it hard for Hollywood stars to adjust to everyday life.

After a spinach factory is burgled in Basingstoke, police believe they may have found the culprit.

... and Virginia Bottomley performs her famous shadow puppet of a Thai prostitute.

A TRAINSPOTTER'S GUIDE

*H*ave you ever wondered how many programmes have been won by Ian and how many by Paul? Have you ever wondered which guests have answered the most questions correctly? You sad bastard.

Still, you're not alone. Either of you. In response to massive public demand for these and other details too tiresome to mention, teams of highly-paid researchers, working round the clock, have been holding our tea boy's head down the lavatory until he agreed to do all the work for them. Here are his astonishing results:*

ASTONISHING RESULT No. 1

Ian Hislop gets more questions right than Paul Merton. So the reason Hislop's been losing all these years is that he's been accompanied by a gang of piss-poor deadbeats such as **Jonathan Ross** and **Danny Baker**. After all, who else would dare go into battle equipped only with **Derek Hatton**? Merton on the other hand, is revealed not to be the awe-inspiring intellect that everyone took him for, but a struggling numskull with a questionable taste in shirts.

ASTONISHING RESULT No. 2

The Tub of Lard scored more points than Roy Hattersley, registering 37.5 per cent to Hattersley's 22.22 per cent. Obviously this score was achieved with help from his team captain – otherwise the Lard would have been even further ahead.

* Oh all right, they're not *that* astonishing. Mildly diverting, possibly… if it's a Thursday afternoon and you've got nothing to do. And it's raining. And your wife's left you. Oh please come back, Brenda, I promise it'll be different this time.

SOME RATHER LESS ASTONISHING RESULTS

Top of the pile was *Punch* editor (now ex-*Punch* ex-editor) **David Thomas** who spent so many weeks revising for his appearance that all discipline in the *Punch* office evaporated and the magazine closed down a few days afterwards.

Journalists occupy most of the places in the top fifteen although there are exceptions. Smart-arsed Cambridge know-it-alls **Clive Anderson** and **David Baddiel** are clearly better equipped to present *Channel 4 News* than **Jon Snow**. Although Jon Snow did once go out with Anna Ford, which despite several sad begging letters neither of the other two have yet achieved.

Rory Bremner didn't know many of the answers, but fortunately was able to do an impression of someone who did. **John Sessions** didn't know many of the answers, and unfortunately was only able to do an impression of a seventeenth-century Spanish novelist.

Names in the second group include **Caroline Quentin**, who got more than her husband Paul Merton – their professional life thus mirroring their private life with uncanny precision.

Neil Kinnock was the most successful MP (not a sentence you come across very often), coming in twenty-seventh, a mere twenty-five places below his usual result. A stack of Labour MPs were right behind him (and that's another sentence you don't come across very often).

The feminine touch graced the third section with **Maureen Lipman**, **Mariella Frostrup** and **Frank Bough** all making an appearance.

Everyone who appears in the bottom half of the table suffers the added indignity of being shown to possess less guile, wit and intelligence than a cheaply moulded plastic tub full of processed animal fat. Names in this category include **Edwina Currie**, **Stephen Fry**, **Cecil Parkinson** and **Salman Rushdie,** all singled out here purely for amusement value. Rushdie's score was particularly disappointing; you'd think a man in his position would have a few spare minutes to flick through the *Daily Star*.

The real stars of the show occupy the bottom few places. **Vitali Vitaliev** has a good excuse, in that only one of the questions in his show was in Russian, while **Arthur Smith** has a good excuse, in that he's totally useless. Pressed for an explanation of *his* poor performance, **Bob Geldof** informed us: 'F*** off, you c***s'.

Pipping chirpy cockney ignoramus **Danny Baker** to last place was Ian Hislop's predecessor at *Private Eye*, **Richard Ingrams**, with a sparkling display of ineptitude. Ingrams now edits *The Oldie* magazine, which is attempting to fill the gap in the market left by *Punch*. Clearly, he has a lot to learn from David Thomas – or is it the other way round?

Overall Results

Series	Paul	Ian
1	6	–	2*
2	8	–	3
3	9	–	2**
4	5	–	5
5	6	–	2
6	7	–	2***
7	5	–	3

* Ian wins first ever programme. Paul never looks back

** Ian 2 – 1 up after 3 games. Paul wins series by record margin.

*** In last show of series, Ian tries sitting on Paul's side, wearing tasteless shirt. Paul wins show by record margin (13 points).

Swots

		%
1	David Thomas	84.61
2	Francis Wheen	66.66
3	John Diamond	65.38
4	Fiona Armstrong	63.64
5	Baz Bamigboye	62.50
6	Alan Coren	61.53
7	Clive Anderson	60.00
8	David Baddiel	59.09
9	Meera Syal	58.82
10	Jon Snow	57.14
=11	Lesley Abdela / Amanda Platell	55.56
13	Germaine Greer	54.40
14	Rory Bremner	52.77
15	Ian Hislop	50.68

Not as clever as they thought they were

		%
=16	Hugh Dennis / Robert Harris / Trevor Mc Donald / Maria McErlane / Bob Monkhouse / Gill Pyrah / Caroline Quentin / Jan Ravens / Steve Steen	50.00

Not as clever as *we* thought they were

		%
25	Paul Merton	49.30
26	Maureen Lipman	46.88
27	Neil Kinnock MP	45.00
=28	Chris Evans / Mariella Frostrup	44.44
30	Tony Banks MP	43.18
31	Sir Rhodes Boyson MP	42.85
32	Michael White	41.66
33	Tony Slattery	41.11
34	Martin Young	40.62
=35	Nick Hancock / Gerald Kaufman MP	40.00
=37	Frank Bough / Chris Tarrant	38.89
39	Rory McGrath	38.70
40	Jo Brand	38.24
41	Griff Rhys Jones	37.87

Clearly something fishy going on

		%
42	The Tub of Lard	37.67

Unimpressively mediocre

		%
=43	Kathy Burke / Kevin Day / Harry Enfield / Eddie Izzard / Kathy Lette / John Stalker	37.50
49	Donna McPhail	37.22
50	Edwina Currie MP / Jerry Hayes MP / Clare Short MP / Sandi Toksvig	36.36
54	Frank Skinner	36.21
55	Tony Hawks	36.11
56	Douglas Adams	35.00
=57	Anne Robinson / Salman Rushdie / Sir David Steel MP / Mark Thomas	33.33
61	Cecil Parkinson MP	31.82
62	Ken Livingstone MP	30.35

Miserable failures

		%
=69	Joan Bakewell / Russell Davies / Annabel Giles / Simon Hoggart / Charles Kennedy MP / Alexei Sayle / Norman Willis	30.00
70	Peter Cook	29.41
71	Kate Saunders	29.16
72	John Wells	28.57
73	Stephen Fry	27.78
74	Richard Littlejohn	27.50
=75	Stephanie Calman / Dillie Keane	27.27
77	Jonathan Ross	26.79

News Cretins

		%
=78	Jack Dee / Bob Geldof / Derek Hatton / John Sessions / John Simpson / Arthur Smith / Jimmy Tarbuck / Vitali Vitaliev	25.00
86	Roy Hattersley MP	22.22
87	Craig Ferguson	20.83
88	Steve Frost	20.45
89	Danny Baker	20.00
90	Richard Ingrams	19.67

ODD ONE OUT

JOHN McGREGOR

MUHAMMAD ALI

PRINCE CHARLES

DEBBIE McGEE

They're all Muslims, aren't they? John McGregor used to be called Yusuf Abdullah. Prince Charles was Cat Stevens. Debbie McGee isn't.

The words 'straws' and 'clutching' spring to mind.

They're all members of the Magic Circle, except Muhammad Ali, who was expelled from the British Magic Society for giving away tricks of the trade. Ali once boasted that he could raise himself several inches off the ground with a simple piece of footwork. Yes, it's called jumping.

Prince Charles is a member of the Magic Circle. He's particularly keen on the 'sawing your wife in half' trick.

John McGregor MP is apparently an expert mind-reader. Asked by reporters if he'd answer a question or two about it, he replied, 'On my seventh birthday, yellow, upside-down and Alan Titchmarsh.'

Paul Daniels' wife, Debbie McGee, is in the Magic Circle in her own right. She complains, 'They think Paul only married me for the way I look.' Well, it certainly wasn't the other way around.

Paul Daniels has got a bloody big Rolls Royce and it's parked outside the BBC. The registration number's 'MAGIC'.

Is it really? How tragic.

You probably can't get one that's got CRAP written on it, can you?

IT'S THE
PRIVATISATION

❶ When he was Secretary of Transport, Sir Norman Fowler privatised National Freight. Now, by an astonishing coincidence, he's a director of National Freight.

❸ In his position as Secretary of Trade and Industry, Lord Young was in charge of regulating Cable and Wireless. Guess what? By an amazingly happy accident, he then became chairman of Cable and Wireless!

> HELLO & WELCOME TO 'THE MONEY PROGRAMME'

❷ As Secretary of State for Energy, Peter Walker was responsible for the privatisation of British Gas. As luck would have it, Peter is now a director of British Gas!

> DON'T YOU JUST LOVE BEING IN CONTROL?

❹ The odds against winning the big prize on the National Lottery are quite astronomical – but not as astronomical as the odds against Kenneth Baker's wife being on the board of Camelot, the company appointed by the Government to run the lottery!

> ...AND THE WINNING TICKET IS ...MY WIFE'S!

Believe It or Not!

5 During his stint as Trade Secretary, Norman Tebbit steered through the privatisation of British Telecom. And now, by a million-to-one chance, he's on the board of British Telecom!

ARE YOU ON 219 3000?

NO, I'M ON **DOUBLE THAT!**

7 When it came to awarding the contract for running Britain's first privatised prison, top-notch security firm Group 4 got the job. Who says lightning never strikes twice? Certainly not Sir Norman Fowler, then Tory Party Chairman and director of Group 4!

THE WOLDS REMAND CENTRE PROP: GROUP 4.

6 Industry Minister Giles Shaw was the man behind the privatisation of British Steel. Now you're not going to believe this, but Giles was subsequently selected – at random – to become a director of British Steel!

HELLO? I'D LIKE TO ORDER A LARGE STEEL SAFE – A **GERMAN ONE** IF POSSIBLE.

8 Of course, the Labour Party would never stoop to handing out jobs running privatised industries to its MPs. They prefer to hand out jobs running nationalised industries. Congratulations Richard Marsh (British Rail), Alf Robens (National Coal Board), Bob Mellish (London Docklands), Lord Beswick (British Aerospace), Ted Short (Cable and Wireless), etc, etc.

HEY, WHAT ABOUT **US?**

LIB DEM

HOW TO DO A VOICEOVER IN **7** EASY STEPS

by the man who fills in when Robert Powell's away

Step 1

Become a well-known television personality. Admittedly, this first hurdle is perhaps the trickiest.

Step 2

Before you know it, offers of work will flood in. Timotei shampoo, Crest toothpaste, Findus Menumasters, New Radion, those horrible Nat West Bank ads, Cooper's Creosote ... the world is your oyster. Simply turn up at the voiceover studio at 9.00 am and make sure there's plenty of room in your wallet.

Step 3

Always be scrupulous about what you will and will not advertise. Refuse to have anything to do with any company unless they promise to hand over an enormous sum of money.

Step 4

Always try to say the name of the product as if you are making love to a beautiful woman. If you are having trouble visualising this, the ad agency can usually provide a beautiful woman for you. Although if you do take up this option, be careful not to end the ad with 'I'm sorry, this doesn't usually happen'.

Step 5

Now let's put those lessons into practice.

'Serbia, land of peace …

'For two thousand years the master tobacco farmers of Serbia have tended their golden harvest. Dried by the fresh easterly winds from the Chernobyl plateau, Serbian Nuclear Tobacco comes in two sizes …

'Regular and Children's Starter Pack.

'Serbian Nuclear Tobacco. For you, your family and your family's family.'

Step 6

Collect your expenses. The cheque will follow in the post, along with the deeds to a small island in the Caribbean.

Step 7

Go home.

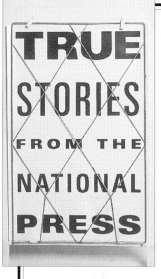

SNIPNOSIS

Patient Andy Bryant has had a vasectomy operation under hypnosis, without any anaesthetic.

He's certainly got balls. Or, he did have until very recently anyway.

Before the operation, Mr Bryant's doctor, Tim Black, said, 'If it does go wrong he will experience a lot of pain in a part of his anatomy which is very close to his heart.' Although it would have to have gone very wrong for it to be close to his heart.

The operation consisted of a single incision in the scrotum, after which the two sperm-carrying tubes were heat-sealed with a soldering iron. His genitals are no longer able to fertilise, but they can now pick up Radio 4.

MAN WITH AN EAR IN HIS LEG

Channel Tunnel worker Pat Neary lost his left ear in a disco fight and, in an effort to save it, doctors transplanted it onto the upper part of his leg, where it had to stay for five months.

Surgeons at East Grinstead Hospital supposedly broke the news to him by saying, 'A word in your thigh, Mr Neary.'

It was predicted that his sex life would be restricted over the following five months, but what there was of it would sound great.

Mr Neary was due back at work in the tunnel soon afterwards, but wearing the world's largest pair of headphones.

LAUGH? I NEARLY SUFFERED A MAJOR AFFECTIVE PSYCHIATRIC DISORDER

Dr Richard Bentall, a psychologist at Liverpool University, has proposed that happiness should in future be classified as 'major affective psychiatric disorder, pleasant type'.

Dr Bentall believes that the only sane people are those depressed enough to think their friends are talking about them behind their back. Because according to the doctor, your friends invariably *are* talking about you behind your back.

In his report, Dr Bentall argues that laughter can seriously damage your health. No wonder the Head of BBC Comedy is looking so well.

After years of experimental study, Dr Bentall has concluded that 'there is clinical evidence of a link between happiness and bodily indulgence'. Most people could have told him that when they were sixteen.

As a result of the professor's findings, the endings of several fairy tales have already been rewritten: 'And so the Prince and Princess lived neurophysiologically disinhibitedly ever after.'

YOU MUST BE DENTAL, DOC

Munich police are baffled by an unidentified dentist who breaks into people's houses, cleans and fills their teeth while they sleep, and then disappears without trace – a sort of dental lone ranger. The people of Munich are now asking 'Who was that masked orthodontist?'

Of course it's the reverse of what happens on the NHS, where if you want any work done you have to break into the dentist's.

In a bid to cut waiting lists, NHS patients who need a lot of expensive bridge work doing have been advised to rent a ground floor flat in Munich, and go to sleep with the light on and their mouths open.

Altogether the mystery dentist has completed about £10 000 worth of work. With the strength of the Pound against the Mark, that works out at about one filling's worth.

There is some doubt as to whether he's a real dentist, as none of his victims say they felt any pain. Evidently he gives them a powerful anaesthetic before drilling and polishing their teeth. How he gets them to rinse their mouth out with pink squash whilst they're asleep remains a mystery.

REFORMED GANGSTERS TOE THE LINE

Tokyo doctors are offering to graft toes onto the hands of reformed Japanese gangsters who have cut off their little fingers in mob initiation rituals.

This surgery enables them to shake hands like a normal person, although they do tend to fall over in the process.

The operations are part of a scheme by the Japanese authorities to introduce reformed gangsters back into society and get them jobs in business. So next time you do a

Medical history is made as a woman gives birth to a man on a bicycle.

deal with a Japanese businessman, have a good look between his fingers for those telltale signs of athlete's hand.

Apparently mobsters' qualities of obedience, loyalty and aggressiveness make them ideally suited to business life, combining, as they presumably do, the ability to get on with clients, to stick with them through thick and thin, and if things don't go well, to kill them.

THE COG THAT'S A BIG WHEEL IN OUR FUTURE

Scientists have perfected a tiny cog – small enough to be held by an ant (see picture below) – to form part of a miniscule vehicle that travels through the human bloodstream, seeks out trouble spots and finds solutions. Rather like a sort of microscopic Lord Owen, only it finds solutions.

The idea is an echo of the film *Fantastic Voyage*, where a shrunken medical team was injected into a patient to neutralise a blood clot. A treatment now sadly only available to patients on BUPA.

The invention is based on a minute Japanese car, fully functioning but smaller than a grain of rice. Unfortunately though, it suffered a setback when it was left unattended-near an artery, and some bacteria smashed the back window and nicked the stereo.

Faster than a speeding pullet!

THE A340 Airbus is having frozen chickens fired at it at 500 miles per hour in an attempt to avoid the problems that dogged the old A320 Airbus. That old problem of hitting rock-solid chickens at 30 000 feet.

Frozen chickens were chosen to simulate eagles and vultures that could strike the plane during a flight. They're the eagles and vultures that fly around trussed up with string, paper frills on their feet and their heads rammed up their bottoms.

An Airbus spokesman explained: 'They explode on the windshield, and we can see what the bones do and how the skin is splattered.' Vegetarians are up in arms and are demanding they fire aubergine bakes at them instead.

Of course, anyone who's eaten on British Airways wouldn't wait for a chicken to hit the windshield – they'd be so pleased to see something edible go past, they'd grab it for their dinner.

Breathe life into plants

IT'S been discovered that plants are so clever that they can communicate with each other, and that when chopped down or attacked a plant emits a high-pitched warning squeal audible only to other plants.

However it's not clear as yet what form these warnings take – 'Duck'? 'Run for your life'? 'Don't move'?

Most developed of all is the bright red and green Venus Fly-trap which apparently also has taste – although with those colours it's hard to agree.

The Venus Fly-trap can count up to two – which scientists say in theory makes it cleverer than a computer. Yes, but can it book airline seats to New York?

Sobering news for hamsters

EXPERIMENTS into alcoholism have been going on at Harvard, with the aid of some Syrian golden hamsters.

Apparently the Syrian hamster can happily get through the equivalent of a case of wine without showing signs of inebriation. That's apart from the traffic cone on its head and the three giggling gerbils in the back of the Escort.

Syrian hamsters' tastes are all the more remarkable considering that they're offered simply a mixture of pure ethanol with water. Whereas most hamsters, of course, prefer it with bitter lemon.

You'll never believe who's on the line

A NEW type of telephone has been invented, called the Truth Phone, which lights up when the person on the other end of the line is lying.

For instance, when you ring BT and the operator says, 'Sorry to keep you waiting.'

The phone retails at £2499 but the manager of the store that sells them said it was excellent value for money – whereupon every phone in the shop exploded.

The Times tested the phone on MPs Bill Cash and Austin Mitchell. In order to prime the machine, they initially had to be asked questions such as: 'Is today Friday?' 'Is the month April?' and, 'Are you wearing a tie?' If you asked John Major those questions, he'd think you were striking up a rather interesting conversation.

THE TRUTH PHONE – SURVEY RESULTS

An illuminated score of 40–50 represents a truthful answer, and a score of 70-80 implies that the subject is telling porkies. Tory MP Bill Cash scored as follows:

'IS TODAY THURSDAY?'	'YES.'	44
'IS YOUR NAME BILL CASH?'	'YES.'	41
'IS JOHN MAJOR GOOD FOR BRITAIN?'	'YES.'	77
'DO YOU WANT TO BE PRIME MINISTER?'	'NO.'	102

That sweet smell of success is … $C_2O\,H_{24}O$

ARTIFICIAL aromas have been invented to entice people into shops.

The smells include coconut oil in travel agents, cut grass in greengrocers, and leather in car showrooms. Let's hope Sock Shop never joins the scheme. And quite what sort of aroma Anne Summers has in her shops doesn't bear thinking about.

The purpose is to encourage customer loyalty by using a corporate perfume to express a company's personality. So you'll presumably get the smell of hopeless farts in Dixons.

$C_2O\,H_{24}O$ is the chemical formula of the most popular smell – that which bonds new-born babies to their mothers. As opposed to the smell that bonds new-born babies to their nappies. $S.H._1T.$

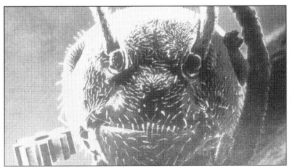

Ants everywhere are now hoping that someone will devise a miniature phillishave.

NEWS JUST IN

There's good news in the capital, as Her Majesty The Queen launches National Smile Week.

In a rare moment of relaxation, Dr Hilary Jones looks back on a hard year's work.

There's uproar as the Security Services raid Margaret Thatcher's fridge.

A newly-issued photograph suggests that Richard Branson may have been subjected to his most humiliating smear yet.

... and London Zoo announces the birth of the world's first showbiz chicken.

ODD ONE OUT

CLIFF RICHARD

BISHOP OF GALWAY

SAMANTHA FOX

STEPHEN FRY

ANSWERS

I used to go out with the Bishop of Galway.

That's not the answer, Paul, true as it may be.

That's me, behind him there, look. He's just said to me out of the corner of his mouth, 'Lose yourself, there's a photographer in the room.'

The Bishop of Galway, Dr Eamonn Casey, is the odd one out, as all the others are avowed celibates.

Cliff Richard, curiously, says he nearly got married three times. Must have been a bit irritating for his fiancée.

Stephen Fry admits to being 'half gay' (presumably the bottom half) and is quoted as saying, 'Everyone has got their bottoms exploding with blackberries. It's good to bring it out in the open.' If his bottom's exploding with blackberries, it's not surprising he's celibate.

Former Page Three girl Samantha Fox also refrains from having full sex. That must be a blow for her boyfriend.

The Bishop of Galway, on the other hand, fathered a lovechild by Anne Murphy, who describes their first encounter in her book: 'His eyes lit up. I unfastened my blouse and bra, and let them fall to the ground ...'

Why was he wearing her blouse and bra?

We may never know.

He used to take me to the pictures you know. I'd sit in the back row and hold his crook.

A WASHING LINE OF MY OWN

with Angus Deayton

ANGUS SAYS: My favourite washing line has to be the Hozelock 'Lift and Click' Heavy Duty A322. Line sag is a perennial problem when hanging out washing, but the Hozelock's three line tension positions go a long way to eradicating this washday headache. The A322 has a corrugated aluminium frame, a handy 3.30 m turning circle and a tough styled hand-grip for comfortable use. After a heavy boilwash of all my silk suits, up to 130lb of washing pushes the double outer line system to its limit, but I know the Hozelock's durable soil spears will always hold firm. I recommended this line to my old pal Helen Atkinson-Wood, and before I knew it the whole KYTV team had bought one too.

LIFE*style*CHOICES

MY KIND OF GUN

with Ian Hislop

IAN SAYS: When it comes to top-of-the-range weapons of mass destruction, the Supergun™ stands head and shoulders above the rest. One hundred and seventy-one feet long, the smooth steel of the barrel, tapering from twelve inches thick at the base to one inch thick at the business end, means that from its launch-site at Iskandariyah the gun can hit Tel Aviv and Tehran with equal ease. And what's more it's British made – with the full knowledge and approval of Her Majesty's government. The gun comes complete with export licences waived and with removable cover-up. Here's what the man in the street* has to say about the Supergun™:

* Whitehall.

'We can't possibly allow the facts to come out in the trial. Sign this.'
(SIR N.L., WESTMINSTER)

'I'm not signing anything. Those businessmen could end up in prison, then we're all for it.'
(M.H., WESTMINSTER)

'So where do I sign?'
(K.C., WESTMINSTER)

'Oh, all right then, you've convinced me.'
(M.H., WESTMINSTER)

ME AND MY AGRICULTURAL FUNGICIDE

with Paul Merton

PAUL SAYS: Of course, when you're looking for an agricultural fungicide you're spoilt for choice, but to my mind you'd be hard pressed to beat Herbifendazine. It's terrific for seeing off brown foot rot and ear blight, covered smut, leaf stripe, loose smut, net blotch, mildew, rhynochosporium, yellow rust, and brown rust in winter barley. Naturally, protective gloves are a must, any seed you treat with it can't be eaten and it's highly dangerous to fish. But nit-picking aside, it's got to be the finest systemic benzimidazole (MBC)-type fungicide on the market. And if you've got any Gammasan 30 left over (so long as Mr Robinson from next door hasn't been on the scrounge again!!) you'll find Herbifendazine a fully compatible mixer.

OF THE STARS

'Er ... I was on holiday at the time, oh yes.'
(J.M., WESTMINSTER)

'I'm sorry m'lud, it seems I've been economical with the actualité. Fancy a shag?'
(A.C., WESTMINSTER)

How NEWS Reaches Your Screen

We follow a major story from its inception to its appearance on HAVE I GOT NEWS FOR YOU.

It may look simple – a few seconds of video tape, a quip or two and another major news story is encapsulated for the nation. But what you, the viewer, *don't* see at home are the weeks, even months, of hard work put into every story by a team of dedicated professionals. We now pay tribute to those men and women.

THE MAASTRICHT TREATY

– how it got onto HAVE I GOT NEWS FOR YOU.

---

481 AD Tribes of itinerant Franks head south from the forests of Northern Germany. The defence forces of Roman Gaul prove insufficient to repel the invaders. Elsewhere across Europe, similar events are occurring as Huns, Alans, Visigoths, Ostrogoths and Vandals forge a new fragmented European order.

c.550 AD A Church is built by the River Meuse in what is now known as the province of Limburg. Around it grows the town of Maastricht. Disputes break out in the streets over how to pronounce the town's name, leading to the famous Diphthong Riots of 573.

1939 AD Adolf Hitler sets out to achieve a united Europe. Winston Churchill vows to stop him.

1945 Churchill leads Euro-sceptics to victory.

1990 Jacques Delors sets out to achieve a united Europe. John Major vows to stop him.

1991 John Major signs Maastricht Treaty for the Unification of Europe.

10th December 1991 All over Europe, the continent's journalists are mobilised for action. Ron Jenkins, Head of BBC Television Foreign Newsgathering Outside Broadcast Network Resource Planning and Management, calls his staff together for an urgent briefing. They are all being sacked to save money. Twenty-seven accountants are taken on to administer the sackings.

11th December 1991 After a crash course in how to pronounce Maastricht, the BBC's man-on-the-spot, Martin Priddle, jets out on the first available flight to Belgium. On arrival he is informed that Maastricht is in Holland.

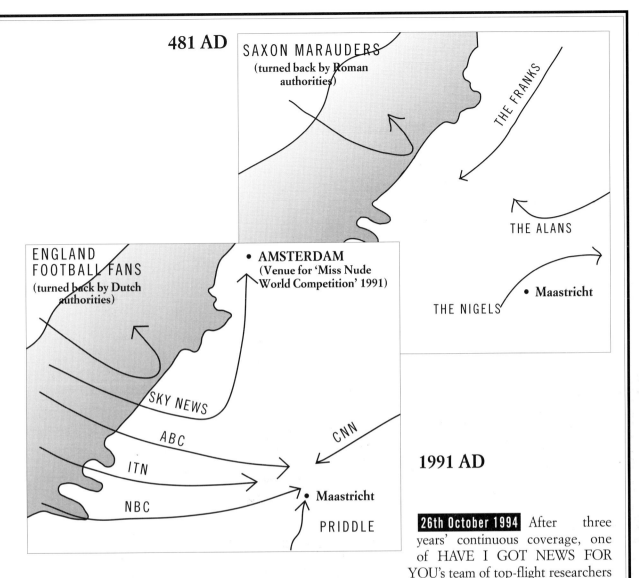

481 AD

SAXON MARAUDERS
(turned back by Roman authorities)

THE FRANKS

THE ALANS

• Maastricht

THE NIGELS

ENGLAND FOOTBALL FANS
(turned back by Dutch authorities)

• AMSTERDAM
(Venue for 'Miss Nude World Competition' 1991)

SKY NEWS

ABC

ITN

NBC

CNN

• Maastricht

PRIDDLE

1991 AD

12th December 1991 Priddle arrives in Maastricht to find that nothing of any interest whatsoever is happening. Back in Britain, the airwaves are immediately cleared for a 24-hour special. Using the very latest technology, pictures of the doors of several identical office buildings are relayed to your screen.

13th December 1991 – the present The FA Cup Final, Wimbledon and Test Match Cricket are abandoned in order to show more pictures of identical doorways. BBC Radio 4 is scrapped to make way for a Rolling Maastricht Channel. A full-scale model of Maastricht town centre is constructed in Peter Snow's sandpit.

26th October 1994 After three years' continuous coverage, one of HAVE I GOT NEWS FOR YOU's team of top-flight researchers says, 'Er … shouldn't we do something about this Matschriicht thingummyjig?' A question is born.

Production Day Four million hours of news footage are boiled down to one shot of a doorway. A question is devised for Angus which gets straight to the heart of the matter: 'Paul and Roy, this is yours …'

The Show The tape is played in. The audience awaits. 'Oh how should I know,' replies Merton, before going on to make several rude remarks about the chairman's suit. Centuries of history have been brought to a natural conclusion. A grateful nation is finally enlightened.

ODD ONE OUT

ELTON JOHN

ROBERT MAXWELL

FRANK WARREN

JIMMY HILL

ANSWERS

Did you see that thing Frank Warren said about Terry Marsh? He said that their relationship came to an all-time low when Terry Marsh was accused of shooting him.

It is bad for relationships.

Promiscuity and shooting are two of the things that break up more relationships than anything else.

The odd one out is Frank Warren, as all the others have been, or still are, the chairmen of soccer clubs, whereas Warren attempted to buy Luton.

Elton John, as chairman of Watford, was responsible for discovering Graham Taylor. So he has a great deal to answer for. That was in the days when Watford were great and Elton was bald. Somewhat oddly he now has a full head of hair and Watford are rubbish. A sort of 'Samson and Watford' story.

As chairman of Fulham, Jimmy Hill has years of experience, yet still retains the fresh, youthful innocence of someone who knows bog-all about anything.

When Robert Maxwell was chairman of Derby County, he claimed to have pulled off a miraculous achievement in getting crowds of supporters through the turnstiles. Of course, a truly miraculous achievement would have been if crowds of supporters had got *him* through a turnstile.

You know Robert Maxwell died on November 5th – Guy Fawkes Night. So, Guy Drowns Night.

Do you think in years to come children will gather round big pools of water? … And when will they ever learn that a guy is a thing with trousers stuffed with newspaper, not a teddy bear with a jumper on?

Some of them use footballs for heads – as if Guy Fawkes looked like that. 'I don't know his name, mate, but he looked like a football.' So at the identity parade you've got all these blokes and a football.

It's not a great disguise, is it?

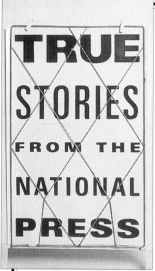

TRUE STORIES FROM THE NATIONAL PRESS

Ban these cereal chillers

THE REVEREND IAN COOK has claimed that the plastic figures given away with Frosties have 'overtones of the occult and represent demons'.

There are apparently sixteen to collect, with names like Elbow Witch, Swamp Beast and Bishop Fish. Certainly the idea of ordaining Michael Fish is pretty evil.

The vicar has complained that each packet contains a grotesque two-inch figure that terrorises children – rather like a shrivelled Jimmy Savile.

The effect, according to the vicar, is to transform breakfast into a satanic ritual. So don't be surprised if your toaster starts reciting the Bible backwards, and your boiled eggs spin round and round, spewing spinach everywhere.

There's no nookie in Heaven

THE POPE has announced in a sermon that 'There will be no sex in paradise'.

Asked by a street cleaner how we would pass the time, the Pope said: 'There will be no need to exercise the act of procreation. We will just watch and watch.' Sounds rather kinky.

Lapsed Catholic Bernard Manning is quoted as saying, 'If I get to heaven, a few of my old girlfriends will be delighted there's a sex ban.' Most of them were probably praying there was a sex ban when they were on Earth.

I do tricks ... just like Jesus.

MAGICIAN Paul Daniels has alleged that Jesus Christ was just like him. Bald and from the Midlands, presumably.

Experts are now investigating the possibility that Christ broke bread at the feast of Cana, turned water into wine ably assisted by the lovely Debbie McGee, and ended by saying 'And that's magic!'

Daniels claims that anything Jesus did, such as walking on water, he can emulate in the twentieth century. Forty days in the wilderness would be a good start.

Galileo wins 359 years too late

GOOD news for seventeenth century Italian astronomer Galileo. Galileo, who asserted that the earth orbits the sun, was pardoned recently by the Catholic church, which after 359 years has admitted that it was wrong to condemn him. Although the West Midlands Police are still reserving their judgement.

A Church Commission set up thirteen years ago has only just confirmed that the earth is not the centre of the universe. It would have been quicker, but it took them twelve years to work out that it wasn't flat.

Pope John Paul II apologised for the medieval and primitive attitude of his predecessors, and said Galileo's severe punishment would only have been justified if he had done something really wrong, like wearing a contraceptive.

Apparently his full name was Galileo Galilei. Mr and Mrs Galilei must have pondered long and hard over christian names for their son before coming up with Galileo. Of course, no one would be stupid enough to do that nowadays. It would be like a Mr and Mrs Magnusson, for instance, calling their son Magnus.

A child who has overindulged in Kellogg's Frosties falls prey to demonic possession.

The gay rights that angered Archbishop Carey

A GAY prayer book is due out, despite the opposition of the Archbishop of Canterbury, containing gay versions of ecclesiastical ceremonies.

There's a gay marriage service: 'Do you take this man… and how often?'

And there's even a gay divorce ceremony, in which parting lovers are urged to bury a seed in a bowl of earth, though not in the onanist sense of the word.

So anyone who moves in with a new gay partner, and finds every bowl in their kitchen is full of geraniums – beware.

The ceremony requires divorcing couples to: 'Take a mug, plate, or another piece of china, and smash it to show the end of their life together.' A spokesman for Relate, the marriage guidance council, said, 'Why do they need a ceremony? Most people do that as a matter of course.'

Saintly path to a profit

THE VATICAN is to sell Papal souvenirs because they say the Catholic Church is poverty stricken. That's poverty stricken in the 'owning several million acres of land across the world' sense of the word.

A Vatican spokesman warned that in the years to come, some of the Catholic clergy will almost certainly be 'strapped for cash'. The Bishop of Galway was the first to volunteer when he heard the news.

The Vatican has insisted that the new range of goods will in no way be cheap, tacky and exploitative. On the contrary, they will be extremely expensive, tacky and exploitative.

Products include: Last Supper aprons, Stigmata transfers, and wine 'n' wafer flavoured condoms. Perforated, naturally.

Kosher monkey

HARD-LINE Rabbi Josef Ovadia has suggested that in order to avoid any kind of activity on the Sabbath, Orthodox Jews should train monkeys to perform basic household tasks. It is feared he's been watching too many PG Tips commercials.

According to the Rabbi, the Halacha (the Ancient Jewish Law) stipulates that 'Man shall work for six days and on the seventh he shall rest and let a monkey do the hoovering'. Of course, they will have to find gentile monkeys – Jewish monkeys might refuse on religious grounds.

Among the simple tasks forbidden on the Sabbath are switching on lights, turning on the cooker and driving cars. So the next time you're cut up at the lights by an Orang-utan in a Mercedes, blame the Rabbi in the back seat.

The Bishop of Durham personally takes part in the church's new-look go-ahead Easter pageant.

God is sent three tax demands

Lambeth Council has admitted to sending three Council Tax demands of £521 each to the Church of St John the Divine in Brixton, addressed to God the Father, God the Son, and God the Holy Ghost.

They even offered God the chance to pay it off in instalments. Fortunately they didn't ask him to list his other premises.

Lambeth has now had scores of frivolous Council Tax applications, ranging from Adolf Hitler to Donald Duck. The Council has complained that it is very hard to tell the difference between a genuine householder and Mickey Mouse. A three-year study group has now been set up to find out which one lives in a house in London and which one is an American cartoon character with big black ears and a squeaky voice.

AND NOW, LET US PAY

THE Reverend Derek Sawyer, vicar of St Aldates, Gloucester, has announced that he intends to introduce charges at his church.

Individual services will cost £4.50, or £9.00 for the Nativity service starring Frank Bruno and Anita Dobson.

If you're taking communion at St Aldates don't be surprised if you're asked if you want to see the wine list.

In defence of his scheme, the vicar said, 'Just think how much people spend in McDonalds.' Although he admitted that you have to weigh up whether you want eternal salvation and spiritual redemption or a Filet-o-Fish and French Fries.

Sorry, the end of the world isn't nigh

LEE JANG LIM, a leader of the Christian church in Korea, has apologised for the world not ending. Lim had previously announced that he and his followers would ascend to heaven and that the end of the world would soon begin.

Curiously, Lim turned out to have banked £2 500 000 worth of his followers' money, in bonds not due to mature until 1995. Just as well for him that the end of the world was mysteriously postponed.

Bizarrely, Australian scientists concede that Lim may be right, as they say a six-mile-wide ice-cube is heading for the earth. Oliver Reed has already started working on a seven-mile-wide gin and tonic.

The giant ice-cube is actually due to arrive on 14th August 2116. A Croydon woman who's just fallen downstairs is particularly worried because she's been promised an ambulance that day.

Experts predict there'll be scorching temperatures, culture and learning will be wiped out and gangs of thugs will roam the debris. A bit like a Club 18-30 holiday.

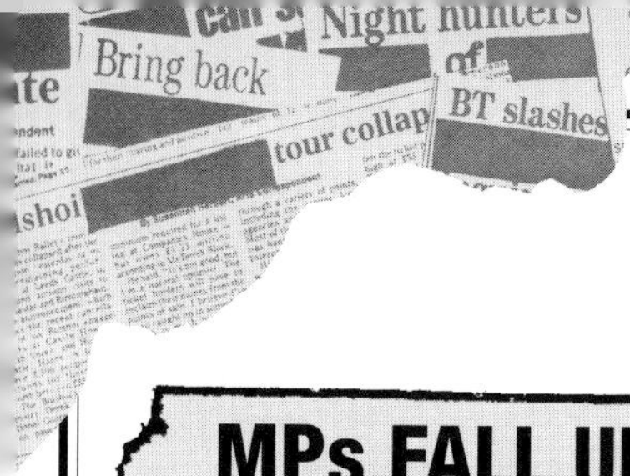

Missing Words

MPs FALL UNDER ▮▮▮▮

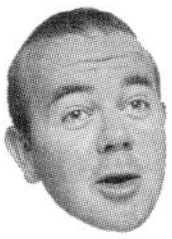

Secretary?

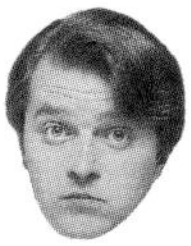

It's three words. It must be Number 37 bus.

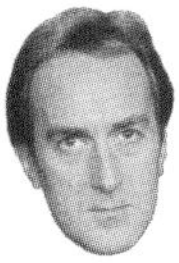

No.

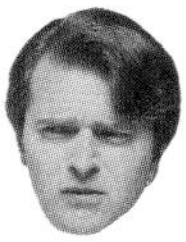

Number 78 bus? 64? 29?

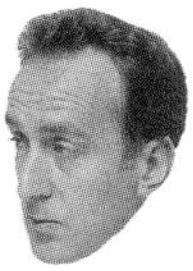

No. Put buses from your mind.

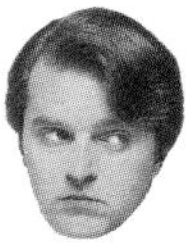

4.15 from Paddington? 6.15?

ANSWER: Spell of star witnesses

▮▮▮▮ COULD BE STICKY FOR CHARLES

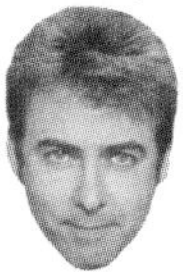

Camilla Parker-Bowles, if he plays his cards right.

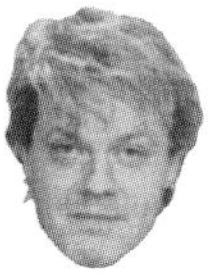

Re-entry?

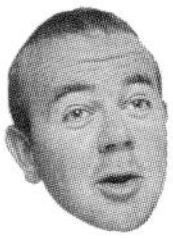

Same thing.

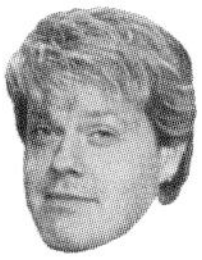

I'm talking about space.

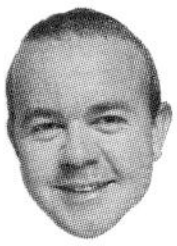

Large lollipop?

ANSWER: TV tapes

DINOSAUR SETTLES ▮▮▮▮

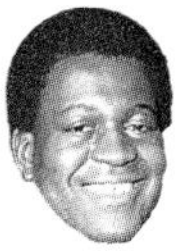

In Essex?

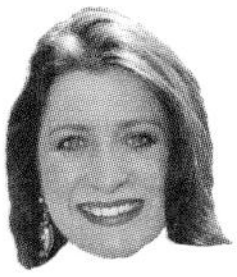

Family argument?

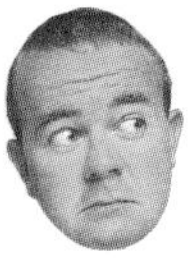

Stomach? 'Feel a bit dicky? Have a dinosaur.'

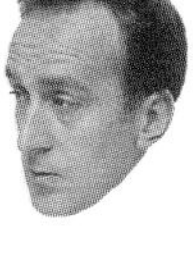

I'll give Caroline one …

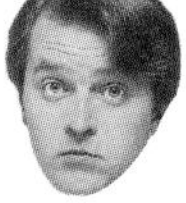

Pardon?

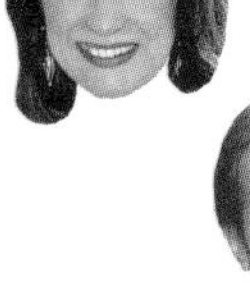

Thank you very much.

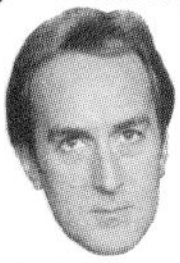

The answer's Divorce Row, fittingly enough.

ANSWER: Divorce Row

WINNER: YES, I'VE FOUND ▮▮▮▮

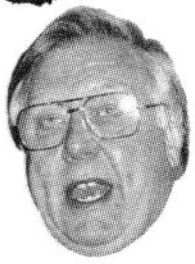

Underpants?

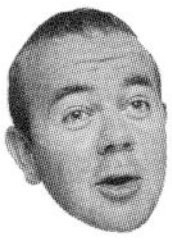

I've found my own true love – it's myself.

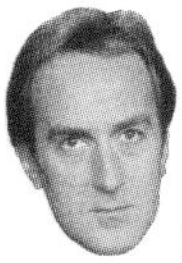

New Love is the answer.

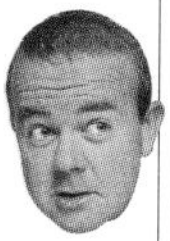

It's funny how he finds a new love every time he's got a film coming out, isn't it?

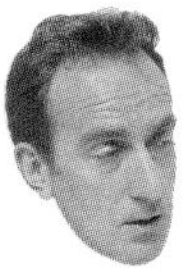

Isn't that libellous?

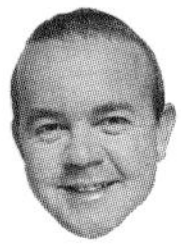

No.

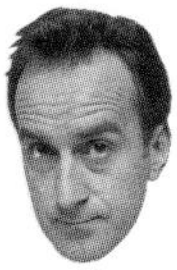

In that case, yes, it is funny how that always happens.

ANSWER: New Love

QUICKFIRE CAPTIONS

'*If I get rid of the other two, how about it?*'

'*Hello, this is the Prime Minister. I'd like to report a faulty mirror.*'

'*I wouldn't like one of them swimming up me arse.*'

NEWS JUST IN

Following a planning blunder in Middlesborough, an office block is built over a car park without informing the drivers who regularly use it.

Jon Pertwee has been chosen to replace the Andrex puppy.

A new photograph reveals why the Germans supported the franc and not the pound in the recent financial crisis.

Recently discovered evidence casts doubt on historians' traditional theories of how Crusaders made their way to the Holy Land.

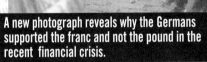

... and after reading that injections of cow hormones can make your lips bigger and sexier, the Duke of Edinburgh gives it a try.

ODD ONE OUT

HARVEY PROCTOR

JULIAN CRITCHLEY

GARY LINEKER

CECIL PARKINSON

Have you scored forty-eight goals for England?

No, I haven't.

Some of those people left the Tory Party after scandals, but that obviously isn't the answer.

That's a bit below the belt, isn't it?

The odd one out is former MP Harvey Proctor, as all the others have modelled shirts, whereas Harvey Proctor makes them, and indeed lifts them … onto the shelves of his new shop.

Gary Lineker is quoted as saying, 'I'm quite fussy when it comes to clothes.' So naturally he models shirts for Littlewoods.

Lord Cecil modelled shirts last year, leading his colleague Julian Critchley to remark caustically, 'He is presumably appealing to the older shirt-buyer.' As opposed to Mr Critchley, who appeals to absolutely nobody.

I never modelled shirts.

Ah, well …

Do you believe him? Think of his record! 'The NHS is safe', 'I didn't model shirts' …

I've always fancied modelling underpants. You know, where you're standing next to another bloke wearing underpants, pretending to look at something far-off: 'Look! There's the bloke who's got our trousers.'

Youngsters are so grey

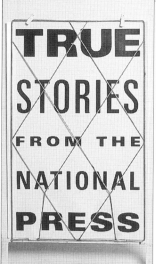

A recent survey has revealed the existence of a new generation of 'Major's Children'. That must have come as a bit of a shock to Norma. Major's Children are said to be a gentle generation, who 'put people before Porsches'. That's not gentle, that's positively dangerous.

Nowadays, apparently, schoolchildren's main interests are saving the environment, stopping animal cruelty and mixing with family and friends. Whatever happened to good old smoking in the toilets and pulling the wings off insects?

Like the Prime Minister, Major's generation are said to be sober-looking and serious, whereas Thatcher's children were smartly dressed and ready to work all hours. Thank God Michael Foot never got in or there'd be loads of sixteen-year-olds going round with donkey jackets and false teeth.

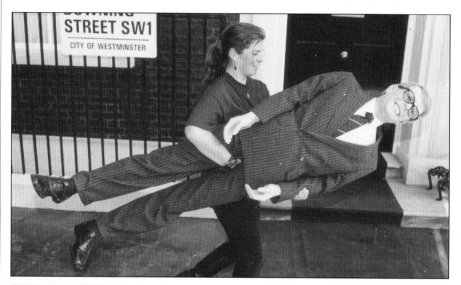

John Major is rushed to hospital after experiencing his first orgasm since 1968.

It's Heil Thatcher

BRITISH politicians are in shock at the news that some irresponsible vandal has painted a Hitler moustache on the portrait of Mrs Thatcher in the House of Commons coffee room.

It must be the first time she's been touched up since Cecil left.

Betty Boothroyd has launched an investigation to identify the culprit. She says the whole of Parliament will have to stay behind until someone owns up.

A restorer has now been employed to get the portrait absolutely accurate again. He's going to add jackboots and an armband.

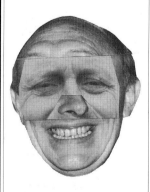

Police have now issued an identikit of a man seen near the portrait on the day of the crime.

Half a fish finger diet

A £10-a-week menu for the poor has been drawn up by the Ministry of Agriculture. The diet includes a quarter-slice of processed cheese a day, a tablespoon of baked beans a day and half an egg a week. But who would want to risk the other half after it had been sitting around for seven days?

The diet also suggests eating half a fish finger. You can keep the other half by in case you have a dinner party.

The government said the Second World War had shown that people could survive quite healthily on this sort of diet. Of course the War also showed that people could survive being bombed by the Luftwaffe every day, but it doesn't necessarily mean we want to go through it all again.

Experts are now claiming that if you add up all the ingredients in the £10 diet, it actually comes to £30. Obviously Norman Lamont was in charge of the final calculations.

MP gets a busted flush

JOHN PRESCOTT MP got a surprise soaking when a toilet that he visited on a London to Leeds express flushed *up* instead of down, saturating him from head to toe.

Anyone who finds the idea of the Deputy Leader of the Labour Party being drenched by a jet of his own effluent remotely amusing should be ashamed of themselves.

British Rail, for their part, said the waste pipe had been misconnected. It should have gone straight to the buffet car.

Who kin that be?

THERE was embarrassment for Neil Kinnock at Marks and Spencer after staff failed to recognise him when he tried to pay by cheque.

Playing down the incident, an M & S worker said, 'We actually prefer customers like Mr and Mrs Kinnock to VIPs.' Not so much damning with faint praise, as just damning.

It's also been revealed that the same shop opens especially early for Virginia Bottomley, Mrs Thatcher and other Tory luminaries. So Maggie gets in and Neil doesn't. Sounds familiar.

Privacy protest over the man who came unstuck

OBJECTIONS have been raised in Parliament over the press treatment of a Mr John Bloor, who accidentally super-glued his buttocks together. Of course, that's a rather different sort of 'crack and glue' epidemic from the one affecting the nation's youth.

The story appeared the next day under the headline, Our John's Gone Potty, And Glued Up His Botty. And the *Financial Times* wasn't the only paper to cover it.

Mr Bloor's MP, Joe Ashton, is now demanding that the right to privacy in these kinds of circumstances should be enshrined in the statute book. So, look out for the 'Superglueing of Buttocks' Private Members Bill.

The accident occurred because the glue which Mr Bloor's wife had been using to mend a shoe was in the bathroom next to his haemorrhoid cream. As a result of the mix-up, the shoe has now been admitted to hospital with an anal disorder.

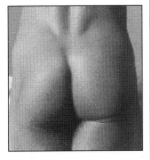

An entirely gratuitous photo of a pair of buttocks.

MPs' sexy phone line unplugged

AUTHORITIES have moved to stop calls to sexy 0898 numbers being made from the House of Commons. BT's profits are expected to plummet.

Evidently MPs have been using these services rather a lot, but knowing their regard for protocol, they probably still get their secretaries to actually make the call. 'Miss Fanshawe, get me "Busty Big Bertha – Mine Are Real Whoppers" on the line for me, would you?'

As a replacement, BT have now offered a rather more wholesome 'House of Commons Chat Line'. Twenty-four MPs are hooked up at once, then one talks for three hours while the others fall asleep.

Mellor hit by punchline

CONTROVERSY continues to surround David Mellor, this time following his departure from studio twelve at Granada TV, when he was jumped on by a man.

Now he knows how Antonia de Sancha felt.

The irate member of the studio audience pushed him over, knocked his glasses off and attacked him, following a discussion programme called *TV Violence*. Just as well it wasn't *Sex Talk* or God knows what he would have done to him.

The show posed the question 'Is gratuitous violence justifiable?' And, where David Mellor's concerned, the answer would surely be a resounding yes.

David Mellor at last finds an object of lust that won't go running to the papers.

Killer at Commons

THERE were red faces in Westminster when it was revealed that a drug-running international criminal had managed to merge seamlessly into the House of Commons.

Working there as a waiter, the twenty-seven-year-old Jamaican turned out to be a hitman wanted for several murders all around the world, a drug dealer wanted for smuggling crack and cocaine, and an illegal immigrant travelling on a false passport.

But apart from that his credentials were absolutely impeccable.

His job involved serving tea and coffee to MPs; suspicions about his drug trafficking past were first aroused when he asked a politician who took sugar if he wanted one line or two.

BEHIND THE DESK

What the viewer never sees

ODD ONE OUT

LORD WHITELAW

MARK THATCHER

GARY NUMAN

GAVIN NASH (AGED 9)

ANSWERS

Mark Thatcher got lost in the desert – and his mum cried, didn't she?

Everyone else was laughing.

Then everyone cried when they found him.

If you know who the little boy is, you'll know the answer to the question.

Has he got the other three locked in a cupboard?

The answer is that all of them own guns, apart from multi-millionaire, Mark Thatcher, who's been accused of flogging them to Middle East dictatorships. Presumably when he goes on business trips to Saudia Arabia he thinks he's just helping out a fellow European country.

Gary Numan is famous for owning a huge arsenal of guns. Just as well, as he's not famous for anything else any more.

Lord Whitelaw went on a shooting party in 1984 and managed to shoot not only one of the beaters but his host Sir Joseph Nickerson. A spokesman said: 'I think Sir Joseph would like it kept private.' Bearing in mind where the pellets struck, I should think there's every likelihood of that.

Gavin Nash is one of a number of small boys who have been granted a shotgun licence. Incredible isn't it? You have to be sixteen to have sex, eighteen to watch other people having sex, but only nine to be given the wherewithal to blow someone's brains out.

Arms deals involving Mark Thatcher were being investigated in 1992 by British journalist Jonathan Moyle, who was found dead in a Chilean hotel, having received a lethal injection. The British Embassy refused to help local police and even tried to make out that Moyle died of masturbation.

Makes you proud to be British, doesn't it?

THE ART OF COURTROOM DRAWINGS

A DO-IT-YOURSELF GUIDE

Y ou see them every night on the TV news. Instant sketches that capture the vibrancy of the British legal system, drawings that add a vital element of mystery to an otherwise uninteresting court report. Who is that man on the witness stand? Martyn Lewis just said it was George Michael. So why does it look uncannily like Demi Moore? Or is it John Selwyn Gummer? No, wait a minute – it's Fred West! Possibly.

These drawings may look as though they've been dashed off unthinkingly in five minutes. But in fact it takes several years of practice to get this bad.

Here's how one of Britain's top courtroom artists, David Aldridge, produces an amazing quickfire likeness of popular singer and High Court superstar George Michael.

1 Advance preparation

David Says: 'The whole process starts months before the trial with the selection of the materials. I use pastels on brown parchment, as the rough flocked texture ensures that all one's outlines must be broad, bold and woefully inaccurate.'

2 Technique

David Says: 'Very often defendants are nervous and shift around in the witness box. The answer to this is simple. A swift half or nine at the Three Ferrets and the whole courtroom will appear to move with them. Your confidence will soar and your drawing will become unfettered, uninhibited and, above all, unlike the scene before you.

As every aspiring courtroom artist knows, perspective is a vital element of your preliminary sketch. Here's a little tip: hold a pencil at arm's length; then draw everybody – no matter how far away they are – the same size as the pencil.'

3 The Personal Touch

David Says: 'Now is the time to add those little individual flourishes that mark your work out as your own. In line with many other court artists, my personal hallmark is a mysterious brown smear around the heads of my characters, as if they've attracted a swarm of flies or have just been pushed through an adjoining wall. Remember, the court adjourns at 4.30 pm and your picture is due on air at 9.15 pm. The pressure's on – you've got less than five hours to check your picture for any recognisable features and excise them.'

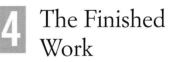

4 The Finished Work

David Says: 'Transmission time – you've made it! Draw like this and you too can work for BBC News. It's fun, it's rewarding and it certainly beats my old job at the pork butcher's.'

TIM BELL'S
Believe It or Not!

1 Bell once said that he wanted the BBC to fail because it was arrogant and biased. Not unnaturally, he then accepted a contract to promote the Beeb, suddenly convinced it was the finest broadcasting organisation he'd ever accepted a five-figure fee to promote.

3 Timmy was deeply offended by press reports linking him to the Pergau dam scandal. Admittedly he advised the Malaysian government, who commissioned the dam, the Conservative Party, who agreed to give aid for the dam, and GEC who are building the dam. But at no time has Tim represented the little man who sells hotdogs by the side of the dam.

2 Bell won the contract to boost Margaret Thatcher's image, partly the result of a supposed ability to flirt with her. On that basis, he should have won a medal never mind a contract.

4 It was Tim who masterminded the official D-Day celebrations – in their original form – which had to be scrapped after veterans protested that they were tasteless and degrading. In his defence, Tim said it would have been a very moving moment when thousands of Mr Blobbies waded out of the sea, onto the Normandy beaches.

OFFICIAL D-DAY SPAM FRITTER COMPETITION.

He's one of Britain's highest-paid Public Relations Consultants, the man who fashioned Mrs Thatcher's image. So what's gone wrong with his own?

5 It was Tim Bell who advised David Mellor, at the height of his sex scandal, to pose for a disastrously hypocritical photograph with his family. So, if you ever see the Pope pictured in *Hello* relaxing with his wife and kids, you'll know whose idea it was.

6 Another to pay for Tim's services was Chilean fascist, Hernan Buchi, the favoured candidate of mass-murderer General Pinochet. Buchi promptly lost the election – apparently his slogan 'Vote for me and I won't electrocute your testicles' somewhat let him down.

7 Tim has advised the business career of Mark Thatcher. And it's thanks to Tim's genius for public relations that no one has ever made an entirely unjustified connection between Mark's immense fortune and international arms dealing.

8 Tim has also helped fashion the image of the fabulously successful Canary Wharf, Guinness fraudster Ernest Saunders, honest Terry Venables and Coal Board chief Sir Ian McGregor, who once appeared before TV cameras with a plastic bag over his head. Surely Tim didn't advise Stephen Milligan as well?

NEWS JUST IN

After Ken Livingstone wins London's top newt-breeding prize, competitors allege that he may have used steroids.

Mikhail Gorbachev denies he is having an affair with Denis Thatcher.

There's confusion at the Dominion Theatre, as Madonna's after-show entertainment arrives.

. . . and the friends of Norman Lamont gather for a ballet charity gala.

HAS ANYONE SEEN TIM BELL?

ODD | ONE | OUT

JOHN MAJOR

MICHAEL HESELTINE

PETER LILLEY

PRINCE CHARLES

ANSWERS

Prince Charles is the only one who's wearing a hat?

An astute observation, if entirely irrelevant.

Three of them have got their hands, or bits of their hands, in the picture and one of them hasn't.

Well I hope that's his finger sticking up there.

The odd one out is Prince Charles, as the other three have, between them, been pelted with the various ingredients of a quiche. Namely eggs, flour and tomatoes.

In Toxteth, Michael Heseltine's forehead was hit by eggs and tomatoes on a steamy hot August day. Just as well they didn't hit his hair or they might have started frying.

Peter Lilley was struck with flour by students at the LSE and John Major won the 1992 election after having eggs thrown at him. Of course, strictly speaking, you need a large metal dish to make a quiche, so if any students are reading this, do bear this in mind next time he's in your area.

In Australia, Prince Charles was not attacked with food, but an anti-royalist did suddenly run at him, spraying an aerosol as he went. 'People just can't help acting on impulse.'

I said Prince Charles, I should get a point.

But it's not your go, is it?

That's a bit anti-social, Salman. Dear me, you should get out more.

Going anywhere nice for your holidays this year?

IF IT SPLITS, YOU'RE ON A HAYDN TO NOTHING

A new musical condom has been invented which, if it bursts, warns you to withdraw by playing Beethoven's Fifth.

Although Schubert's 'Unfinished' would seem more appropriate.

The invention could lead to an innovation in pubs, where the condom machine will be able to double as a jukebox.

The Italian inventor, Lino Missio, said, 'When a condom breaks you need to be warned urgently.' He has spent years perfecting the invention on himself, and is now celebrating with his wife and fourteen children.

A survey last year revealed that 20 per cent of all men say condoms are too small. The other 80 per cent are telling the truth. Researchers were also intrigued by the surprisingly low percentage of complaints that condoms were too big.

Tax break for busty stripper as US judge sizes up her assets

A judge has given a stripper £2000 worth of relief. Which makes a change from the other way round.

Exotic dancer Chesty Love won a tax rebate on the cost of her silicone enlarged breasts, because oversized physical attributes enhanced her stage act. Apparently, the Inland Revenue is now writing out a cheque for a million pounds to Tom Jones.

Chesty Love's 56 FF-sized breasts weigh in at 10lb each, which, in European terms, means just under 5kg, and, in British builders' terms, means 'pfwooooah!'.

Awarding the claim, the judge said that Ms Love's new breasts were also responsible for the fact that she and her husband were no longer very close. Although it would be difficult for anyone to be very close, by the sound of it.

A leaked photograph suggests that the police may have embarked on their own version of the Madonna book.

ALL THE VICE GIRLS LOVE AN ABSEILER

The so-called 'loose women of Cardiff' have decided to exchange their stockings and stilettos for stout walking shoes.

Spot the Ball Competition.

As part of a charity scheme to introduce them to new experiences, the prostitutes are to be taken to the Brecon Beacons where they will be lashed together with rope for rock climbing, and pull on rubber wet suits for canoeing. Sounds a bit like a busman's holiday.

One of them said, 'We said no to abseiling because we thought it meant being pulled in a boat.' They seem to have confused it with shagging a sailor.

Participating prostitutes have been told to bring £3 and a lunchbox. Hopefully none of them will misunderstand that one.

A South Cardiff police sergeant said: 'With the amount of money these girls charge, they could afford their own day out.' It's still not entirely clear how he knows how much they charge.

TART WATCHDOG

A national watchdog body, OFFPRO, has been set up by vice queen Lindi 'Miss Whiplash' St Clair, to monitor complaints against prostitutes.

They're a bit like OFTEL, except that they deal with people complaining they're *not* getting dirty phone calls.

Although OFFPRO has been set up to protect the consumer, it's still difficult to imagine Lyn Faulds Wood getting involved in this sort of watchdog, and telling viewers: 'We took this rotating dildo...'

In fact, the organisation has already had to deal with a number of complaints about prostitutes. One client got only three minutes for his £50, although that's still cheaper than an 0898 number.

Another man handed over £2000 at Victoria Station and didn't even get to meet the prostitute ... although the name of that gentleman has been withheld.

A DUMMY RUN WITH ALBERT, MY SILENT KNIGHT

AN INFLATABLE car passenger, nicknamed Albert, has been designed to ward off the attentions of strange men.

Apparently, perverts have taken to climbing into the vacant passenger seats of cars, beside the driver. Of course, if they're that perverted, sitting on top of the dummy will be a bit of a bonus.

Although Albert is a relatively lifelike partner, they intend bringing out a more lifelike one next year, which gradually falls across you in a drunken stupor and vomits in your lap.

The only question now left unanswered about this inflatable companion is whereabouts the nozzle is.

Albert the inflatable dummy passenger. Rather than modelling him on Mike Tyson or Lennox Lewis, the makers apparently decided that passing nutters would be most terrified by the notion of getting into a car with Bamber Gascoigne.

POSTMAN PORN

POSTMAN Alan Fenney has been found guilty of pushing pornography though people's letterboxes.

His trial will be followed by that of thousands of paperboys who deliver the *Sunday Sport*.

One of his victims was Major General John Irvine, whose wife Mary found him opening a plain brown envelope stuffed with porn. He explained that it must have been sent to him by a postman with a grudge against members of the establishment. An excuse so limp, it makes 'I only shared a bed with him to save £10' almost plausible.

Major General Irvine said: 'My wife Mary wanted to know where they got people to pose for pictures like that.' Worth asking perhaps, but they're almost certainly looking for someone younger.

Matthew Jewell, prosecuting, said: 'Other titled people in the area had pornographic material stuffed through their letterbox.' But their only complaint was that it was two weeks late.

SEX THERAPY FOR MAN WHO FELL IN LOVE WITH A FAMILY CAR

A man named 'George' has developed a close, erotic relationship with his family's Austin Metro.

His parents say they are very disappointed. They were hoping he'd settle down with a nice Bentley.

It all started when 'George' began masturbating inside the car, which presumably makes overtaking rather dangerous.

He was also aroused by Vauxhall Novas, Vauxhall Astras, Fiat Unos and Ford Fiestas. So looking at a transporter must have been the equivalent of a centre-spread in *Health and Efficiency*.

'George' is now being cured using 'Orgasmic Reconditioning Therapy', which gradually substitutes women for cars in his fantasies. Sex is now fine - until the critical moment when he tries to do a three-point turn.

GILLIAN TAYLFORTH road tests the new Austin Metro.

NAKED SPICE TO ARMY LIFE

A bizarre ploy has been devised to test the resolve of our soldiers in mock battles, by littering the battlefield with girlie mags to see how many of the troops would be distracted.

As it turned out, army chiefs said they were unable to tell how many succumbed, as 'Nothing came up in the debriefing afterwards.' Probably a sign that most of them did succumb then.

In a real war, apparently, the enemy might plant a hidden bomb in a porn mag as a come-on, although a spokesman for the Imperial War Museum expressed scepticism. 'The Russians didn't do it in Afghanistan,' he said. In fact, the Russian equivilant would be to leave a bomb cunningly concealed inside a tractor manual.

According to a spokesman for the magazine, 'All the top brass read *Penthouse*. We know as we've had lots of letters from them.' That'll be in the Brigadiers' Wives section.

The Wardrobes of the Stars

by our fashion staff, Tina Blind

You can tell a lot about the way a man dresses by looking in his wardrobe ... obviously. Take a tour round Angus Deayton's wardrobe and you'll be instantly struck by the style, the elegance, the sheer designer quality, and by the fact that you're hopelessly lost, it's getting dark and you can't remember the way back to the exit. Go into Ian Hislop's house and look into his wardrobe and you'll be struck, physically, by Ian himself. Go into Paul Merton's house and look inside his wardrobe and you'll probably find Angus – in the arms of Mrs Merton. To avoid all this trouble, here's a cut-out[1]-and-keep[2] guide to the wardrobes of the stars.

Inside Angus' wardrobe: level four.

[1] Although, to be honest, there's not much point in cutting it out.

[2] Come to think of it, there's not much point in keeping it either. Just throw the whole book away.

CONTENTS	ANGUS	IAN	PAUL
Silk suits (many of them tragically brown)	543 269½	0	½ (pair of Angus' trousers delivered by mistake)
Nondescript woolly jackets and cheap loud ties (non-matching)	0	57	0
Shirts of such unyielding hideousness as to take your breath away	0	0	162
Manchester United kits for sad fantasising in front of mirror	2 (1 home 1 away)	0	0
Full Bishop's outfits	0	1	1 (when Bishop of Galway stays over)
Luminous green rabbit suits	1	1	1
Discarded fish	0	0	13 (7 Hake 3 Cod 2 Rock Salmon 1 Chub)
Lost wardrobe mistresses	7	0	0

'*Return to your constituency and prepare my dinner.*'

'*Puppet squad – nobody move.*'

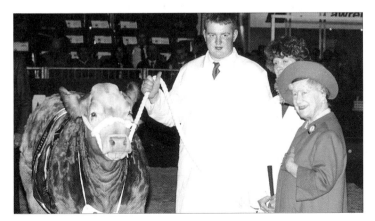

'*Well, if you're sure Madonna's finished with it ...*'

Missing Words

YELTSIN SCORES ███

Cocaine?

Is libellous.

Five goals for Scotland?

Yeltsin scores twelve, if you get him in scrabble.

Is it 140 – a celebrity dart throw on *Bullseye*?

ANSWER: Big win

TEBBIT ATTACKS ███

Rottweiler?

The Pope?

At night?

ANSWER: Lack of common values

MY DAYS AS CLOSET HETEROSEXUAL BY ███

Boy George?

Lloyd George?

Lloyds Bank ... or is it Jason Donovan?

No, obviously not.

I mean he's a heterosexual ... he might have a closet.

Yes, he might be choosing his suits in the morning. 'I'm a heterosexual in a closet.'

Nothing libellous there.

ANSWER: David Bowie

DANGERS OF ███ THE ███ BY PRINCESS DIANA

Kissing the frog?

It is Thomas the Tank Engine?

Dangers of ... overdoing the saintly bit.

ANSWER: Sonic the Hedgehog

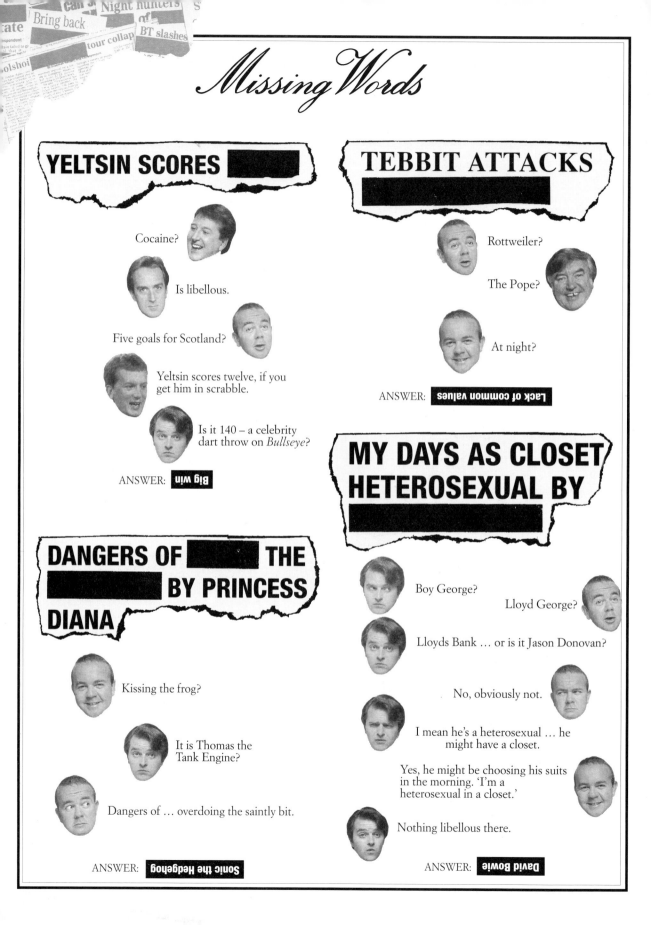

THE ROUNDS THAT NEVER MADE IT

Have I Got News For You may come across as a smooth, seamless, well-structured half-hour's entertainment (oh all right then, maybe not every week), but in fact, a rigorous selection procedure was required to whittle down the number of rounds to the four we know and love today. Here's just a selection of some of the rounds that never made it past the pilot stage.

ODD ONE IN ROUND

RULES: The panellists are shown photographs of four people. All of them have something in common, except three of them.
REASON DROPPED: On grounds of extreme pointlessness.

INTERNATIONAL CRISIS ROUND

RULES: The panellists are required to devise a lasting peace plan that will finally settle a centuries-old dispute, with the help of relevant star guests.
REASON DROPPED: Yasser Arafat storms out of studio following heated nine-hour debate over whether to have Peek Frean or Jacob's custard creams at the tea-break.

NEWSPAPER ROUND

RULES: All contestants required to get up at 5.00 am and deliver newspapers to producers' homes.
REASON DROPPED: Soon rumbled.

LIP-READING ROUND

RULES: Guests are invited to lip-read film footage of the Royal Family relaxing at Balmoral, shot from some distance.
REASON DROPPED: The programme is often repeated before the 9.00 pm watershed.

GUESS WHAT TIME THE REPEAT'S GOING TO BE ON

RULES: Panellists try to guess what time the repeat's going to be on.
REASON DROPPED: Completely impossible.

COVER TO COVER

RULES: The four guests are given *The Times*, the *Telegraph*, the *Guardian* and the *Independent* to read from front to back. First to finish gets two points.
REASON DROPPED: Person reading the *Independent* invariably fell asleep after twenty minutes.

YOU'VE BEEN FILMED

RULES: Viewers are invited to send in their humorous home videos, which are then amusingly linked by an annoying man with a beard.
REASON DROPPED: Legal action by LWT.

SWIMSUIT PARADE

RULES: Panellists parade in their swimwear, to be judged by Richard Branson and Eric Morley.
REASON DROPPED: Industrial action by almost everybody.

BLINDFOLD ROUND

RULES: Blindfolded panellists have to guess a major politician's identity purely by kissing them.
REASON DROPPED: Cecil Parkinson insisted on Frenchies.

PETS' CORNER

RULES: Panellists bring in their pets for a studio discussion.
REASON DROPPED: Sadly axed after Norman Willis' puma ate Charles Kennedy's chicken.

MARIELLA FROSTRUP ON THE BOUNCY CASTLE

RULES: None.
REASON DROPPED: Complaints about Ian Hislop's behaviour.

Incidentally, if you have a new idea for a round for *Have I Got News For You*, why not send it to:

New Ideas For A Round for *Have I Got News For You*

Keighley and District Municipal Refuse Disposal Site

Keighley

West Yorkshire

YB2 3CP

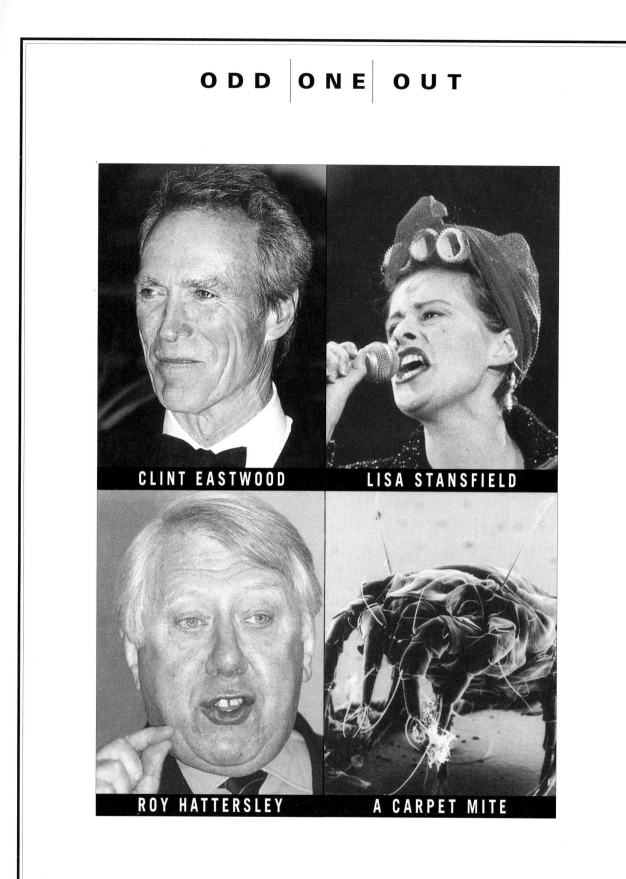

CLINT EASTWOOD

LISA STANSFIELD

ROY HATTERSLEY

A CARPET MITE

Have they all stood for election apart from Lisa Stansfield? Because there was the carpet mite by-election in 1961 in Wolverhampton.

Oh yes, I remember.

The Macmillan Government put up a strong Tory but this carpet mite suddenly came up out of nowhere and said, 'Well, I'm sorry but the local services aren't good enough.'

It got in with a sweeping majority.

And then somebody trod on it, just as it was going into the House of Commons.

The answer is that they all suffer from allergies, except the carpet mite which causes allergies. Although it might suffer from them as well, we don't know. Could be allergic to carpets. Could be having a terrible time.

Roy Hattersley's allergy is to red roses, ironically enough. Be different if he could eat them.

Clint Eastwood is allergic to horses, which is obviously why you never see him in any Westerns.

Lisa Stansfield is allergic to her own saliva …

So whose does she use then?

Roy Hattersley's. He's got plenty.

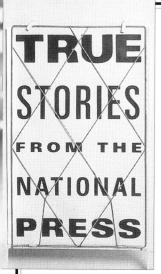

TOMB IT MAY CONCERN

Nine letters have been delivered to corpses at a graveyard near Basingstoke, asking permission to inspect their tombs.

It would have been all right, but three of them actually said yes.

One of the letters, to a Mr Robert Longman, arrived 177 years late. That'll teach them to send it second class.

Mr Longman and his fellow corpses were asked to contact the council if they had any queries, although the last time he queried anything was in 1815, and that was just to wonder what the nice man in the dog collar was doing sitting on his bed.

A council spokeswoman said, 'We might start sending letters to lampposts next.' So, it would appear that European Drugs Week has arrived early in Basingstoke.

SPUDS GET A BASHING

The local council in Cheltenham has banned the sale of all vegetables in the town centre. A spokesman said, 'The sale of dirty potatoes is considered out of keeping with the town's image.' Quite right too. You don't want potatoes with dirt on them, do you? They might look as if they've come out of the ground.

Local Liberal Democrat leader, Alan Stone, also wanted to ban nightclub hypnotists. But after a two-hour meeting with a hypnotists' delegation he told the press, 'I've completely changed my mind ... the hypnotists can stay... and my God, I'm naked.'

EC SAUCE

EC officials have now issued a directive proposing a ban on saucy seaside photos.

Bernard Manning is reported as saying, 'These EC busybodies should remember that laughter makes the world a better place.' He said seaside cards had inspired his own act - presumably that's flat, cheap and dated.

Blackpool sell a million of these cards every year, which might give the Royal Family a few ideas for the Buckingham Palace souvenir shop. They could just print up a few old holiday snaps of Fergie - 'No, silly, I said toe-job.'

EXEMPT - THE HOLY CHURCH OF GNOME

The so-called 'Extremely Reverend William Kibble', a Scarborough postman, has won the first round of his battle to avoid paying council tax on the grounds that he and his wife are members of a religious order dedicated to the worship of garden gnomes.

According to the law, it is possible to exempt yourself from council tax if you can prove that you don't work and that you occupy yourself solely in idle contemplation and long periods of inactivity. As a postman, he's halfway there already.

UNDER THREAT

'MONSTER?
- OCH! YOU SHOULD'VE SEEN THE SIZE OF IT IN MAH YOUTH!'

IS YOUR HAMBURGER MADE IN HAMBURG?

A motion has been passed in the European Parliament forbidding foodstuffs to be called after a place name unless they're actually made in that place.

All french fries may soon have to be made in France, all LA lager may have to come from Los Angeles, and if you go into a restaurant and order a Spanish omelette, you may have to wait rather a long time.

Sandwiches will have to come from Sandwich, wellingtons from Wellington, you'll only be able to wear a Dutch cap in Amsterdam, and you'll only be able to use French letters in Paris. EC experts have advised people to avoid eating in Chechen Ingushetia.

Fortunately for McDonalds, there's no such place as 'Beefburg', and very little chance of anywhere being called 'Quarter Pounder with Cheese, and an Apple Pie that burns your tongue to a crisp and squirts all over your tie'.

DSS APOLOGISE FOR BARE CHEEK

Forty-six-year-old Carol Eshelby, a former bank clerk and victim of Repetitive Strain Injury (RSI) has been advised by the DSS to get a job as a nude model.

The department claims it is only an example of the type of jobs they believe she could do. Others include car park attendant, food taster, and amusement arcade worker - or if she fails the IQ tests for all of them, perhaps a DSS official.

Mr John Daniels of the DSS has now apologised for any upset which the suggestion might have caused. Not at all. Perhaps Mr Daniels should become a rent boy. Apologies for any upset that suggestion might have caused.

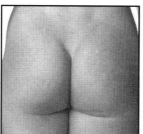

Another gratuitous photo of a pair of buttocks.

'DO YOU KEEP STATIONERY MISS?'
'NO LOVE - I WRIGGLE A BIT.'

'HOW WOULD YOU LIKE TO TRY A LENGTH UNDERWATER?'*

(*The amusing thing is, of course, that he could almost have been talking about his penis.)

TEST RESULTS AT SIXES AND SEVENS

Results of school tests have brought the alarming news that one in three of Britain's six- and seven-year-olds (or, in percentage terms, quite a large number) can't do simple sums or spell basic words such as 'pot'.

They'll soon learn when they want to buy some.

BRITAIN'S SIX- AND SEVEN-YEAR-OLDS

CAN'T SPELL 'POT' (33%)

CAN'T SPELL 'NINTENDO' (33%)

CAN'T COUNT UP TO A HUNDRED (50%)

Three thousand four hundred pupils took the test, which included working out the change after buying a doughnut and a currant bun. It's not surprising they did so badly - it must be forty years since a child bought a doughnut and a currant bun in this country. If only the test had asked how much change they'd have after mugging an old lady of £17.50 and putting the money on Desert Orchid at 11 to 4 on, they'd all have passed with flying colours.

European children are now two years in advance of their British counterparts in all mainstream subjects. But as this recent photograph from a school in Sussex shows, British children are still ahead in the rather more crucial discipline of finding a tree with a bucket on your head.

DEATH THREATS FOR HEAD WHO BANNED PIGS IN CLASSROOM

Headmaster Don Abbey, at the Montgomery School in Birmingham, has banned all reference to the word 'pig' in case Muslim pupils are offended.

Books about pigs such as *Animal Farm, Three Little Pigs,* and Oliver Reed's autobiography are completely outlawed.

The word 'pig' is to be replaced by the word 'panda' - as in 'Salman Rushdie is a stinking panda'.

A Midlands farmer shows off his prize panda.

DINNER LADIES' TV ADS

Schools are to fork out up to £7500 to advertise school meals on television, in an effort to persuade more pupils to eat them.

Alternatively they could make the meals nicer, but that's obviously a bit radical.

The commercial is to feature rap music with the hook line 'School dinners are cool dinners'. Presumably because they were cooked several days earlier.

It's not known how the song goes on – 'Soggy sprouts are far out'? 'Stewed Cabbage is dude cabbage'?

The man who came up with the idea said, 'School meals are good value and essential for the well-being of the school.' Everyone knows that. You can use the gravy to creosote the pavilion and the semolina to repoint the brickwork.

PERSONNEL OFFICERS ARE A WASTE OF TIME

A new study by the LSE has revealed that companies which employ personnel officers actually perform less well than those which don't.

According to the study, 'There's a danger that a personnel department is seen as an external agency which distances it from the rest of the company.' A claim dismissed by the British Institute of Personnel Management from its office in Buenos Aires.

Apparently, there are now so many personnel officers in Britain that they outnumber coal miners ten to one. If only you could convert power stations to run on bullshit.

Ironically, the Government is now forcing thousands of personnel officers on hospitals and Further Education colleges in a deliberate attempt to make them more like big corporations. One expert said: 'Relations between management and staff are now absolutely dire.' So it seems to be working then.

According to the *Independant on Sunday*: 'The research team's biggest problem is to explain why the work of personnel officers is positively damaging.' How about the fact that your career is in the hands of a spotty bureaucrat in a Mr Byrite suit who couldn't do *your* job to save his life?

LOONACY

Children at St Paul's Church of England Primary School in Stafford have been asked to provide their own toilet paper.

The headmaster admitted that he did feel sorry for the children's mothers, having to sew a name tag on every sheet.

Labour have now called for massive increases in education spending, while for the Liberal Democrats, Roy Jenkins demanded a return to the traditional 'three Ws'.

At Home with our Audience It could have been
any of you, but our computer picked out Wilf Northover from Swindon as
the archetypal *Have I Got News For You* viewer. 'I'm a great fan of the show,'
says Wilf, 'and I'm delighted to welcome you into my home.'

KEY

1. My TV, of course. I like to have friends round, to watch my favourite show.
2. A friend. At first he didn't want to stay and watch the programme, but he soon changed his mind.
3. Here's the mind he changed.
4. My dear old mum. She's 117 and Paul Merton's biggest fan. I have to say I'm a Hislop man myself – how does he get away with it?
5. Another friend. This is Gary, who used to drive a TV detector van. It's still parked outside, oddly enough.
6. I'm a keen gardener, especially between the hours of 2.00 and 6.00 am. Whenever Ian loses, I get so cross, but digging helps me relax – and it's amazing what you can find out there!
7. See what I mean! Lovely roses.

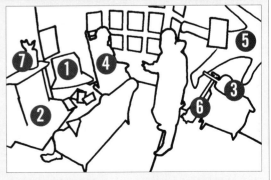

ODD ONE OUT

QUEEN VICTORIA

SIGMUND FREUD

DIEGO MARADONA

PRINCESS MARGARET

ANSWERS

> Is it to do with cocaine?

> Could be. I once tried marijuana. Didn't know what I was doing – I was on coke at the time.

> Victoria looks like a bouncer in a night club. 'Can't go in there, mate, I'm the Queen.' 'Look at that penny, that's me on there. Go on, clear off.'

> I imagine Sigmund Freud experimented with cocaine – hence the appearance of Clement Freud.

All of them have admitted to taking cocaine except, of course, Princess Margaret, who has never admitted to taking cocaine. Because she never has, obviously.

Records from Balmoral's local chemist A.R. Clark have revealed that Queen Victoria bought 'cocaine, opium, heroin and chloroform'. She actually went in for a packet of condoms, but lost her nerve.

Diego Maradona has been arrested for snorting coke. Although he probably just blamed it on the 'Nose of God'.

Sigmund Freud experimented with cocaine and is quoted as saying, 'At first you experience a bitter taste, then you feel light and exhilarated; your lips and palate feel furry and warm.' And before you know it, you're presenting breakfast television with Selina Scott.

> I was horrified to find the other week that my second son is taking drugs. My very best ones, too.

NEWS JUST IN

In Washington, there's concern that Bill Clinton's personal bodyguards may not be blending as discreetly into the background as they might.

After new evidence is found concerning the Birmingham Six, West Midlands police invite them back in for a chat.

Nicholas Fairbairn announces he is to leave politics, having landed the lead role in *Rupert – The Movie.*

After extensive trials, scientists are disappointed with the results of the long-awaited charisma drug.

In Bosnia, army chiefs find it hard to disguise their reactions at the news that Keith Chegwin is to entertain the troops.

BRITISH JUSTICE

❶ The former owner of Walsall Football Club, Terry Ramsden, was found guilty of fraudulently acquiring £90 million of investors' money for his company. The judge decided not to send him to prison because he said he'd read 'moving' letters from Ramsden's friends and colleagues.

❸ After two thugs beat Christian Sollors senseless with an iron bar in an unprovoked attack, Judge Richard Cole decided not to send them to jail. Christian's father Melvyn punched one of the men on their way out of court and swore at the judge. Judge Cole promptly sentenced him to three months in prison. Presumably the fact that Mr Sollors had less than a year to live due to terminal cancer explains the judge's leniency.

> AFTER YOU M'LUD.

❷ Cwmbran youth Vaughan Watkins was found guilty of dropping a crisp packet by a local court and fined £1200. Happily, he had no job and no savings, or the full force of the law might have come crashing down on him.

> MY CLIENT HAS ASKED FOR TWO CIGARETTE ENDS & A RING PULL TO BE TAKEN INTO CONSIDERATION.

❹ Roger Seelig was put on trial for his alleged part in the massive Guinness fraud. £400 000 of his legal costs were paid from the public purse. The judge abandoned his trial because Seelig was 'bewildered' and 'unable to think straight'. So bewildered that he is now a company director of Norman Hay Ltd.

> I AM BEWILDERED, M'LUD.

> YOU'RE NOT THE ONLY ON

Believe It or Not!

❺ Rat-like businessman Roger Levitt was arrested by the Serious Fraud Office on charges of deception totalling £65 million. After a further £1.4 million had been spent bringing him to trial, Levitt changed his plea to guilty to a 'specimen charge' and was sentenced to just 180 hours' community service. He now lives in a £750 000 house. His five children are privately educated.

I FIND YOU GUILTY OF THE SPECIMEN CHARGE OF... ...FAILING TO RETURN A LIBRARY **BOOK** ON TIME.

Would you trust this man?

❻ Jobless youth Paul Powell, sitting in the public gallery, wolf-whistled an attractive female juror as she walked into the court. Judge Geoffrey Kilfoil refused to accept his apology and sentenced him to two weeks in prison.

THERE'S ONLY ONE GORGEOUS BEAST IN STOCKINGS HERE...AND **THAT'S ME.**

❼ Former Guinness chief Ernest Saunders was found guilty of theft, conspiracy and false accounting after a trial that cost the public £20 million. Unlike many top fraudsters, he was sentenced to two and a half years in prison, but was released after just ten months on the grounds of 'pre-senile dementia'. Mysteriously he made an instant recovery, was given £150 000 tax-free by Guinness and now works as a consultant in London and Switzerland.

I SENTENCE YOU TO PRISON.

BUT YOUR HONOUR, I WORK IN THE CITY!

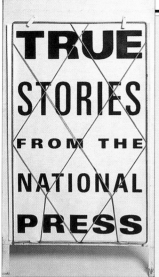

BUSINESS

Ants hold secret to bug-free BT system

British Telecom have announced plans to revolutionise the way they operate their telephone system – by studying the behaviour of ants.

So if your phone starts to play up, just pour a kettle of boiling water down it.

The new BT system is based on a handful of rules that control ants as they forage for food: apparently, if they find food they take it home, if they cross a trail left by another ant they follow the trail until they find food, and if they find nothing they wander around until they do find something. Much the same set of rules that govern Glaswegians and pubs.

According to BT, ants are autonomous software agents on an interconnecting telecommunications network. Curiously, many people have long believed them to be six-legged insects. Suspicions have now been raised as to what sort of substances BT have been spending their profits on.

Talking telephone numbers

Meanwhile, the Chairman of British Telecom, Ian Vallance, has awarded himself an extra £64 000 – described in the press as a telephone number salary, which presumably means he keeps getting the wrong amount.

He now earns £1200 a week more than he used to. Experts say that he could phone Directory Inquiries every day for that. But then, who begrudges the Chairman of British Telecom an extra sixty-four grand a year?

Just about everyone, probably.

Chaos in central London, as news gets around of a cash dispenser that's still got some money in it on a Sunday evening.

Soap wars bubble on

New formula Persil is under attack from the makers of Ariel who claim, somewhat libellously, that it rots clothes. A libel that *Have I Got News For You* inadvertently seems to have repeated. The new powder can get rid of any stain, by the simple method of removing the bit of shirt with the stain on it. Allegedly.

According to Proctor and Gamble, the makers of Ariel, any fabric washed in new Persil develops large holes after just twenty-five washes. Cher has asked for all her clothes to be washed in it twenty-six times.

Unilever, makers of Persil, called a press conference in Holland, where executives produced knickers washed in their new product, which they claimed 'had no holes at all.' So how do you get into them then?

Unilever claim that their rivals are just jealous, because Persil removes heavy soiling better than any other powder. Apparently it was successfully road-tested over the winter by England batsmen in the West Indies.

City loses faith in newspaper's millionaire deal

It was the offer 20 000 readers couldn't refuse, from the *Mail On Sunday*'s city correspondent Adam Faith: if they each sent in £6000, he would turn it into a milion.

The *Daily Mirror* used to run a not dissimilar scheme – except that you sent them a million in pension contributions, and they turned it into £6000.

The over-optimistic scheme has now been abandoned. However, the unusual idea of employing a former pop star as a City analyst has been fiercely defended by the paper's financial editor, Dusty Springfield.

Hand me the big mac please nurse

Burger giants McDonalds are opening a restaurant inside Guy's hospital in London. Hospital chiefs presumably chose McDonalds on the basis that it's the only food that makes hospital meals seem good. A spokesman for the firm said they had already adapted to the NHS ideal – there was now up to a six-month waiting list for a cheeseburger.

Guy's, of course, is the government's flagship trust hospital. Having sold off the catering to McDonalds, they're now selling off the X-ray department to Kodak, and the gynaecological department to Paul Raymond.

Free trip to China

Texaco Ltd have offered a free trip to China for anyone who collects over 30 000 petrol tokens. However, using a Ford Sierra, it's been estimated that you'd have to buy £180 000 worth of petrol. That's enough petrol to *drive* to China and back 200 times. Or enough money to stay in a 5-star hotel in Peking for six months, *and* buy the hotel. Plus buy a new engine for your Sierra, which by this stage will have done a million and a quarter miles.

Tom's will gives toffs the gyp

Cantankerous farmer Tom Bailey has deliberately upset his neighbours from beyond the grave by bequeathing part of his land to gipsies and New Age Travellers.

Neighbours who had spent £100 000 buying their luxury homes told reporters they were 'shell-shocked', as they stood in front of their £20 000 luxury homes.

According to the *Daily Express*, 'Mr Bailey instructed lawyers to set up a camp on his hundred-acre farm.' And if one thing's worse than a camp of gipsies, it's a camp of lawyers.

In the 1968 Caravan Sites Act, gipsies are defined as 'persons constantly travelling, never in one place for more than a few weeks'. Which means that, technically, the Duchess of York is a gipsy.

CAPTION COMPETITION

Thanks but NO THANKS

EVER WONDERED WHY John Major, Margaret Thatcher and Norman Tebbit have never appeared as guests on *Have I Got News For You?* It's because they don't want to. Still, some celebrities at least have the courtesy to write back…

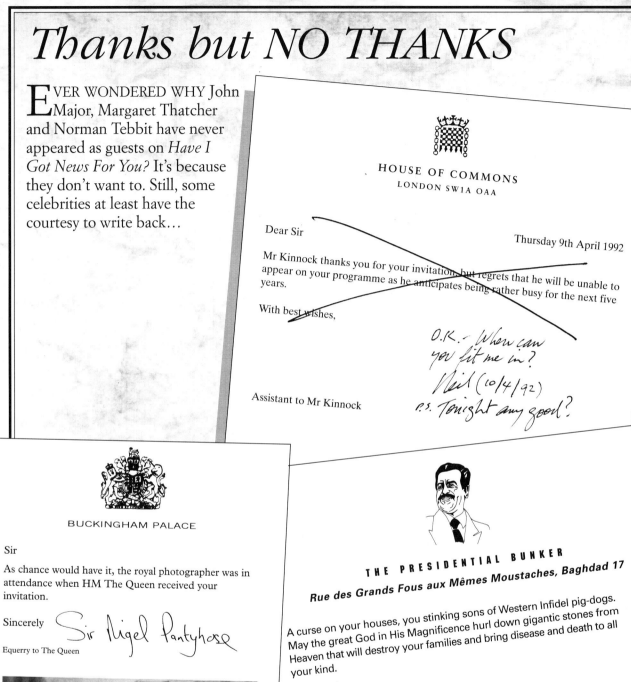

HOUSE OF COMMONS
LONDON SW1A 0AA

Dear Sir

Thursday 9th April 1992

Mr Kinnock thanks you for your invitation but regrets that he will be unable to appear on your programme as he anticipates being rather busy for the next five years.

With best wishes,

Assistant to Mr Kinnock

O.K. – When can you fit me in?
Neil (10/4/92)
P.S. Tonight any good?

BUCKINGHAM PALACE

Sir

As chance would have it, the royal photographer was in attendance when HM The Queen received your invitation.

Sincerely

Sir Nigel Pantyhose

Equerry to The Queen

THE PRESIDENTIAL BUNKER
Rue des Grands Fous aux Mêmes Moustaches, Baghdad 17

A curse on your houses, you stinking sons of Western Infidel pig-dogs. May the great God in His Magnificence hurl down gigantic stones from Heaven that will destroy your families and bring disease and death to all your kind.

Saddam

Saddam

Although I could probably manage the next series if that's alright with you

APOSTOLICA VATICANA

Secretariät of State
Città del Vaticano

P R O F I T E M   A D   I N F I N I T U M

The Vatican

Pope John Paul II, Bishop of Rome, Vicar of Jesus Christ, Successor of St Peter, Prince of the Apostle, Supreme Pastor of the Universal Church, Patriarch of the West, Primate of Italy, Archbishop and Metropolitan of the Roman Province, Sovereign of the State of the Vatican City, wishes to express his thanks and extend his blessings to those who have invited His Holiness to appear on the British Broadcasting Corporation programme *Have I Got News For You.* His Holiness has asked me to convey to you his sincere regrets that he cannot take part in any such broadcast venture following a particularly harrowing appearance on *Fifteen-to-One.*

In nomine patris et filii et in taxem deductibilis

Cardinal Maldini

UNITED STATES

THE WHITE HOUSE

WASHINGTON

Dear Sirs

President John F. Kennedy thanks you for your invitation, but regrets to inform you that he will not be able to take part in *Have I Got News For You,* owing to the fact that he was shot dead in Dallas on November 20th, 1963.

Yours faithfully

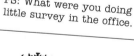

L.B. JOHNSON

pp. John F. Kennedy

PS: What were you doing at the time? We're conducting a little survey in the office.

HOUSE OF COMMONS
LONDON SW1A OAA

Roy Hattersley would be delighted to attend your recording and will be at the studios at 5.00 pm prompt.

Yours sincerely

A. Liar
Assistant to
Mr Hattersley

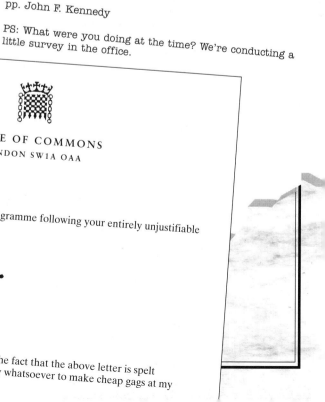

HOUSE OF COMMONS
LONDON SW1A OAA

Dear Sirs

No, I will not appear on your programme following your entirely unjustifiable description of me as a dyslexic.

Yours faithfully

Michael Heseltine

PS: I trust you have taken note of the fact that the above letter is spelt perfectly, giving you no opportunity whatsoever to make cheap gags at my expense.

ODD ONE OUT

HIGHLIGHT

DESERT ORCHID

PRINCESS ANNE

CAMILLA PARKER-BOWLES

Highlight, incidentally, is Prince Charles' polo horse.

Well, Prince Charles has ridden them all, apart from …

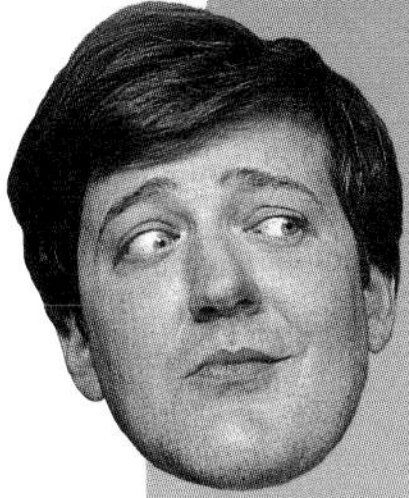

Get out! Get out! Go on – out!

The odd one out is Desert Orchid as all the others annually receive Christmas cards from Prince Charles.

Despite never being sent one by Charles, Desert Orchid receives several thousand Christmas cards from members of his fan club. The annual subscription is ten pounds, for which you get a badge, two newsletters, and a glossy photograph. Sadly, it's not signed, but if you pay a little extra, you can have it trampled on a bit.

Charles, somewhat bizarrely, sent a Christmas card last year to Highlight. The horse said it was 'delicious'.

Princess Anne also gets one from him. As does Camilla Parker-Bowles, to whom he also sends a card.

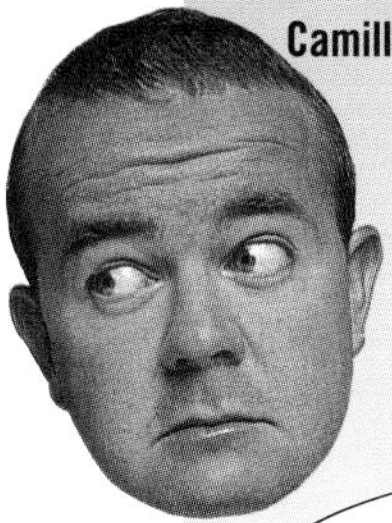

I hope you're going to prove that, Angus.

In court. I shall do.

I wouldn't wear that bow tie because juries go off things like that.

And the brown suit?

Be brown by the time you get there.

NEWS JUST IN

A shock new photograph from the Balkans suggests that John Lennon may be alive and well, and living in Bosnia.

At China's National Portrait Gallery, the prize for best painting is declared a draw.

Suspicions of a cross-party deal are aroused, after Norman Tebbit is seen emerging from a lunch with Roy Hattersley.

England selectors think they may have found a batsman who can face up to the West Indies' intimidating bowling.

... and pictures are finally released showing the wheeze used by Ernest Saunders to secure his release from prison.

In the thirteenth century there was a public offence in England called *scandalum magnatum*. Roughly translated as 'scandalising the mighty', its purpose was to prevent the people from speaking out against the rich and powerful.

In the twentieth century we have the law of libel, which is very different indeed. Oh yes, it is.

Theory and Practice

THEORY

Suppose, for example, you say that a senior Conservative figure is sleeping with his secretary and taking backhanders from a criminal. This seems a pretty innocuous remark to you or me, but the senior Conservative figure in question might consider it to be a bit offensive. He might even consider it to be defamatory.

But is it defamatory in law? There are two questions which lawyers consider in order to establish this – the first dates from 1840, the other as recently as 1924.

(i) 'Does the allegation injure the man's reputation by exposing him to hatred, contempt or ridicule?'

In this case, the answer is probably, 'Yes I hope so'.

(ii) 'Would the words tend to lower the plaintiff in the estimation of the right-thinking member of society generally?'

In the case of a senior Tory, the answer is, 'That is not possible'.

Neither of these answers are in themselves good enough and you may well find yourself being sued for libel. What is your possible defence? Well, you have three options:

(i) You can plead that the words you said or wrote were 'not defamatory'. You could argue that all senior Tory figures have mistresses and bent friends and that it would be defamatory to say that one of them did not.

(ii) You could plead that the words are 'fair comment'. The only trouble about a 'fair comment' defence is that there are strict rules about it, and one of them says that the person making the fair comment must not be motivated by malice. This is fine for me, obviously, but might be more tricky for you.

(iii) The last plea you could try is 'justification'. After fifteen

Ian Hislop's Guide to Libel

years of one party government you might well feel justified in saying anything you like about its members, but the law does not take this view. You

would have to prove that the man got his leg over his secretary and took the money in used notes. This might be quite difficult.

At this stage, you would be advised that there are now two options open to you. Either pay the senior Tory a great deal of money. Or go to court and pay the senior Tory a great deal of money and then pay his lawyers even more.

PRACTICE

I wouldn't recommend this. You won't get any better at it.

QUESTION: Does saying *allegedly* protect you from prosecution?

ANSWER: Many people believe that adding the word *allegedly* to the end of a defamatory remark has the effect of rendering that remark harmless. By saying 'X is a terrific crook, *allegedly*' or, 'Y is a fat old slag, *allegedly*', they believe that they will avoid any risk of being sued. In a sense, for these people, the word *allegedly* has taken on the status of a prophylactic, allowing them to indulge in 'safe libel' while trusting that complete protection is being provided by a tried and tested device.

However, it is only fair to point out that this device is not one hundred per cent safe. In fact some experts believe that it has got a huge hole in it and is likely to fall apart the first time you try it out, leaving you with an unwanted writ to support.

There are two important legal precedents here. The first is from the summing up of Lord Justice Greer in the case of Chapman v. Ellesmere (1932) in which he stated that repeating an allegation was as libellous as making the charge personally. The second is from Paul Merton in the quiz-show of Hislop v. Merton (1992) in which he stated, 'Is that all you have to do? Put *allegedly* on the end? It can't be that easy.'

Greer and Merton are in broad agreement on the subject, as are all other lawyers, and their opinion covers the phrases '*allegedly*', 'it is alleged', 'allegations have been made' and 'I'm-not-alleging-this-obviously-but other-allegers-have-alleged-these-allegations *allegedly*'.

In conclusion, it has to be said that the use of the qualifying adverb *allegedly* in the *Have I Got News For You* manner has as much recognition in English jurisprudence as the use of the qualifying adverb 'not' in the film *Wayne's World*.

Judges are very keen on it. Not. *Allegedly*.

I LOVE EWE

A BEAUTY CONTEST for sheep has been put on, somewhat bizarrely, to amaze the crowds at the Welsh Film Festival.

Of course, if they'd *really* wanted to amaze people, they could have just put on a famous Welsh film.

The judges say that they'll be looking for the usual attributes in the winning contender – grooming, poise, character, and as few straggly bits as possible hanging down the back of their legs.

The evening will divide into three parts when the sheep will be seen in winter fleece, a silk sash and crown, and finally with mint sauce and roast potatoes.

In keeping with other beauty pageants, the victorious Ms Sheep Wales '94 will get the opportunity to travel abroad and meet people. Though if she's got any sense, she'll give France a miss.

Two previous winners of the Ms Sheep Wales title pictured with their rich and influential husbands.

POLLY PUTS THE TELLY ON

IT'S been revealed that TV remote controls operate certain televisions by making a series of unpleasant high-pitched squeaks.

This makes televisions particularly vulnerable when Emlyn Hughes starts talking.

Pet parrots are now learning to imitate these noises and change channels at will. So if you lose your remote control unit, just buy a parrot – always assuming he doesn't want to watch a different programme to you. The biggest problem will be if David Attenborough is on the other side with a steamy wildlife movie, featuring lots of parrots giving each other a beak job.

LAST CHANCE FOR KILLER GUIDE DOG

A guide dog in Germany has so far killed four of his owners. A spokesman for the German Guide Dog Federation admits that it would probably be safer to have a guide sabre-toothed tiger.

The three-year-old alsatian named Lucky (about as appropriate as calling Chi-Chi the panda Randy) guided its first owner under a bus, the second under a speeding train, the third under a car and the fourth off a seaside pier. Obviously he got fed up waiting for the boat.

Lucky is now set to get his fifth owner, who, intriguingly, won't be told about his past. Trainer Ernst Gerber said, 'Basically, Lucky is a damned good guide dog.'

Of course, that could so easily be a German joke – as they are virtually undetectable.

Hedgehogs on hedge of breakdown

The strains of modern life are apparently leading hedgehogs all over the country to suffer anxiety attacks, heart conditions and hyperactive trauma.

Esther Rantzen is believed to be setting up a special 'Hogline' for distressed species.

Some hedgehogs even suffer from sleeplessness. Which is hardly surprising, if every time you cuddle up to your loved one you get stabbed in the stomach. As for their sex life … it doesn't bear thinking about.

The *Sun* newspaper quotes one expert as saying, 'It's sad, because a hedgehog is one of the few animals which isn't harmful to anything – unless you're a slug.' A proviso, there, for the sake of readers of the *Sun*.

THIS PET SHARK IS NO MORE

Pet-owner Tony Finn purchased a basking shark from a pet shop in Hemel Hempstead which continued to lie motionless in the bottom of the tank. In an echo of the famous sketch, he was told by the man in the pet shop that it wasn't dead – 'merely basking'.

Eventually the pet shop owner admitted it might be dead, but claimed it had been killed by the frequent journeys back and forth from the shop.

Mr Finn eventually accepted an out-of-court settlement, a tarantula spider. Clearly his ideal pet would be something that combined enormous sharp teeth and long spindly legs. It's a shame you can't buy pet Janet Street-Porters.

The popularity of sharks as pets is now on the increase. One pet-owner, Sebastian Grant, keeps two lemon sharks in his flat. Apparently they're the world's fourth most dangerous type – although how they measure how dangerous they are must be a long and messy process.

It's the PIG or ME says Wife

Hotelier Stuart Hughes, faced with an ultimatum from his wife that he had to choose between her and his pet pig, Cyril, opted to keep the pig.

Cyril was apparently named after a certain well-known porcine Liberal MP for Rochdale. The pig is now said to be threatening to sue.

According to Mrs Hughes, the pig had taken to strolling into guests' rooms uninvited and jumping into bed with them. Apparently it once had a job as a tour manager with a heavy metal band.

Day of the 3-CLAWED CRAB

A ten-year-old, 8-inch crab has been caught near the outfall pipe of Winfrith nuclear power station in Dorset, and found to have three claws.

Scientists are now trying to find out which way it walks. It probably has the weird ability to walk forwards.

A spokesman claimed that the crab may not have originated from the area around the power station at all. It might just have moved there because it felt at home with the five-eyed lobsters.

Beastenders

Giant tropical spiders, recently escaped from Spitalfields fruit market, are now said to be on the loose in the East End of London. One of them is the Funnel-web spider, which first hides underneath toilet seats and secondly feeds on bananas – an unfortunate and rather painful combination for fifty per cent of the population.

MOTH IS DEAD LOSS

A Hercules moth, one of the largest and rarest species in the world, sadly came to the end of its short life just five minutes before a prospective mate arrived by car from South Yorkshire.

It would have been there sooner but it had difficulty with the hand signals.

Once born, the Hercules moth blooms colourfully for just three days before withering away to nothing. Still, that's longer than 'New Kids on the Block'.

The reason the moth's life is so short is that it has no mouth and therefore can't eat anything – considered by scientists to be no more than a slight flaw in the evolutionary process. This means it has just seventy-two hours in which to find a member of the opposite sex and mate with it. Still, having no mouth should cut out a number of the preliminaries.

The moth has now been mounted – but not in the way that would have made its life worthwhile.

The moth's owner expressed regret that the mating had failed to take place. If only it had succeeded, they could have produced another moth with no mouth and only three days to live. What a wasted opportunity.

ODD ONE OUT

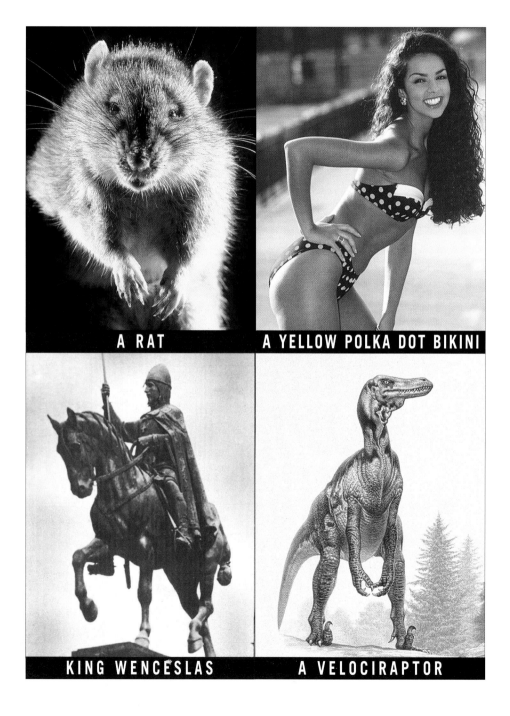

A RAT

A YELLOW POLKA DOT BIKINI

KING WENCESLAS

A VELOCIRAPTOR

King Wenceslas is a Christmas song and that bikini …

… That was a song. 'Itsy Bitsy, Teeny Weeny, Yellow Polka Dot Bikini.'

By the man who looks a bit like you.

Jimmy Somerville?

No, no, he dances like you.

It's that all of them have been the subject of songs, except the velociraptor, which featured in the film *Jurassic Park*. As well as being the most ferocious dinosaurs, scientists say they were highly intelligent. Well, if they were *that* intelligent, how come they didn't kill Richard Attenborough? Must've realised there was a chance of a sequel.

'Itsy-Bitsy, Teeny-Weeny, Yellow Polka Dot Bikini' was a Number One hit for Bombalurina and Timmy Mallet. The bikini, incidentally, was named in 1946, after the small Pacific island which had been targeted by the Americans for an atomic bomb test. Presumably it sounded so much better than 'Polka Dot Hiroshima'.

Michael Jackson recorded 'Ben – Ode to a Rat' in 1972, which featured the immortal lines: '*If you ever look behind, And don't like what you find, There's something you should know, You've got a place to go.*' Yes, Esther Rantzen's Childline.

Good King Wenceslas lived in the tenth century and was believed to be a much-loved and pious example to his people. A bit like Prince Charles, only much-loved and pious. And an example to his people.

Is that a moustache on your upper lip? Because mine has grown out nice and fluffy. Can you get yours to stick up on end?

I certainly can!

Which panto are you two appearing in?

ROBERT MAXWELL'S

❶ Maxwell was so greedy that his staff had to padlock the larder to stop him breaking into it in the middle of the night. Ingeniously, the fat bastard smashed the door down instead.

> MIRROR, MIRROR ON THE WALL, WHO'S THE FATTEST OF THEM ALL?

❷ Maxwell was so vain that he kept a copy of his biography in every room. It was, of course, the nauseatingly obsequious version written by the *Daily Mirror*'s Joe Haines – as opposed to the damagingly accurate version by Tom Bower, which met with a fusillade of writs from the corpulent twister.

> I ALWAYS LIKE A GOOD FAIRY STORY.

❸ Maxwell's publishing company produced the 'World Leader' series of biographies. Paid for by the Eastern bloc, they praised the Romanian psychopath Nicolae Ceaucescu for his 'consistent, tireless activity for the good of his country', and credited the Bulgarian mass-murderer, Todor Zhivkov, with building 'a prosperous and happy nation'. When his publishing staff asked for a pay-rise, Maxwell generously gave them the sack.

BIG BOB'S BOOKS

❹ Maxwell secretly had three ex-policemen bug all conversations in his office and those of his executives. He even listened in on his own sons. A touching display of devotion – most parents give up listening to their children when they reach their teens.

> CAN'T WE GET SOMETHING MORE SOPHISTICATED?

Maxwell

THE OFFICIAL BIOGRAPHY JOE HAINES

Believe It or Not!

5 Maxwell's widow Betty still lives in a £3-million French Château. After years of living the high life on money stolen by her husband, she has had her £300 000-a-year corporation allowance stopped by Mirror Group Newspapers. She complains 'the only person who has actually lost her pension is me'. What a selfish old bag.

WAAAAA!

7 The bloated scoundrel was an agent for the KGB. Although a Czech by birth, when he became a Labour MP he urged the British Government not to help his countrymen in any way against the Soviet troops invading Czechoslovakia. So, not just a liar, a crook and a bully, but a traitor too.

CZECHOSLOVAKIA

6 Former Cabinet Minister Peter Walker received £100 000 in cash, £340 000 in shares and a Mercedes when he left the board of Maxwell Communications, seven weeks before Fatty's death. Despite the fact that Maxwell has been revealed to have stolen millions from Mirror Group pensioners, Walker seems to find it entirely justifiable to hang on to the loot. Wonder what qualities they saw in each other to become colleagues?

IT'S ALL RIGHT, THERE'S PLENTY MORE WHERE THAT CAME FROM.

8 When Maxwell died, John Major described him as 'great' and that 'no one should doubt his interest in peace and his loyalty to his friends'. Douglas Hurd described his disappearance as 'tragic', saying 'the world will be poorer for his absence'. Neil Kinnock said, 'I valued his personal friendship.' And they say our politicians have no judgement …

CAPTION COMPETITION

THE COCKATIEL

(*Nymphicus hollandicus*) prefers to nest by the water's edge. As it is dependent on ripe grass seeds it tends to lead an itinerant life. Generally, the male incubates during the day, but at intervals he may be relieved by the female. So, clearly nothing untoward going on there. A normal, healthy sexual relationship.

THE RED-FRONTED NEW ZEALAND PARROT

(*Cyanoramphus novaezelandiae*) is predominantly a terrestrial bird, with a distinctive and predominantly green plumage. Being a Kiwi parakeet, this one's a bit of a mystery on the masculinity front, but any bird that sires between five and seven young is man enough in my book. Certainly no question of aiming too low in the leap-frog with this fellah.

THE NIGHT PARROT

(*Geopsittacus occidentalis*) is a hardy bird from Western Australia, which

ASK ANY YOUNG GIRL who the hottest bachelor in town is and she'll tell you in one voice, 'Jason Donovan, of course!' The 29-year-old Aussie heart-throb has been breaking young girls' hearts ever since he burst onto the scene some years ago. Now pop legend Jason takes time out to talk about his favourite subject – BIRDS!

JASON DONOVAN'S GUIDE TO BIRDS

feeds on spinifex seeds and broods among the tufts of the spinifex grass. First discovered in 1854, it refuses to this day to be kept by man. Quite right, mate. Good on yer. There's no such thing as free birdseed. He's only after one thing. Watch your tail feathers, little guy.

THE YELLOW-CAPPED PYGMY PARROT

(*Micropsitta keiensis*) burrows into a termites' nest to feed upon the insects and even makes its home there. Its food is heavily mixed with saliva, then exposed to the digestive juices in the parrot's glandular stomach (*proventriculus*), before it enters the gizzard. The sexes are clearly distinguished by differently coloured plumages, which makes the chances of two males 'accidentally' exchanging fluids absolutely zero. Zero, you hear.

THE GROUND PARROT

(*Pezoporus wallicus*) is one of Australia's rarest birds, dwelling chiefly in treeless swamp lands, as the English name Swamp Parrot indicates. The dark down feathers of the young males camouflage them well; even their excreta are black. Not that any of the other young males would dream of coming into any kind of contact with that sort of thing. No way. These are tough, Aussie parrots. What the hell are you trying to insinuate?

ODD ONE OUT

LORD BADEN-POWELL

LADY BUCK

JAMES RUSBRIDGER

DANIEL DEFOE

ANSWERS

> *Daniel Defoe is the only one who said 'Take two bottles into the shower …?'*

> *'… not me, sir. I wash and depart.' I think this is an intelligence question.*

> *You'd better hand it over to us, then.*

The answer is that they were all spies in their time, except for Lady Buck, whose affair with Chief of Defence Staff Sir Peter Harding led to his resignation over feared security leaks.

James Rusbridger was a spy for MI6, who was found dead with ropes around his neck and ankles, wearing oil-skins and a gas-mask. How very odd. No orange.

Baden-Powell was a spy for MI6 and the author of the rather unfortunately titled *Scouting for Boys* – although it was probably just as applicable to MI6 agents as it was to scout masters. Baden-Powell was such an active spy that during the Second World War, Himmler firmly believed that the Boy Scouts were connected to the British Secret Service. Whereas, in fact, as we know, they were just bussed in for parties.

Daniel Defoe is less well-known as a spy than as a writer who helped create one of the most familiar and resonant myths of modern literature. Namely that Robinson Crusoe and Man Friday were just good friends.

> *So Robinson Crusoe was a homosexual was he?*

> *What's a homosexual?*

> *About ten bob a week, isn't it?*

> *It's a long time since you've been out in St James' Park. Goodness me, you'll be lucky.*

NEWS JUST IN

There are allegations that a sordid wife-swapping ring may have started up in Central London.

Somewhere in England, the finishing touches are put to Salman Rushdie's front path.

In Birmingham, police finally arrest the tower block Peeping Tom.

Across the Atlantic, Bolivian television unveils one of the team captains for the South American version of *Call My Bluff*.

. . . and there's good news, as a textbook is spotted in a North London school.

Missing Words

The Day Saddam Tuned Into ▮▮▮

Songs of Praise?

You're not far off.

Derek Jameson?

Sky TV?

No one tunes into Sky TV.

ANSWER: **Blue Peter**

Attention drifts as Kinnock speaks to his ▮▮▮

Elbow? Something like that, anyway.

Heart's content.

Friends?

Yes, almost. Plant is the answer.

What do you mean 'friends is almost plants'?

Plants are our friends, Paul. They turn carbon dioxide into oxygen and keep us alive.

Have you ever met Prince Charles? You'd get on very well.

ANSWER: **Plant**

Tories seek to delay ▮▮▮

Their inevitable dismal failure and collapse?

That'll bring the government down.

Moment of sexual ecstasy?

I won't, thank you.

ANSWER: **Royal Mail break-up**

▮▮▮ is shaken by Portillo.

Milk?

Private parts … in loo?

No one is shaken by Portillo.

Is it glass bowl with Buckingham Palace in it, with snow … ?

ANSWER: **Cabinet unity**

A DAY IN THE LIFE OF THE
TUB OF LARD

Since his appearance as a guest on *Have I Got News For You*, offers of work have been pouring in for Britain's best loved container of animal fat-based cooking product. No day is typical in the Tub of Lard's life, and this is one of them.

Chauffeur and body-guard Reg picks up the Tub for his morning workout at the Pineapple Studios.

Hotfoot from the gym, the Tub pops into Channel 4's Big Breakfast *studio for a quick chat on the bed with Paula, to promote his new sitcom.*

You don't have to look hard at the Tub of Lard to notice that he's a bit thin on top. After talking it over with old pals *Ted Danson and Burt Reynolds, he pops into the private clinic of international weave specialist Mario of Bond Street.*

At Number 10 Downing Street, the Tub of Lard is guest of honour at a special lunch with the Prime Minister. But inevitably, with such a heavy schedule, a certain amount of prioritising is unavoidable, and the less important appointments have to go by the wayside.

Instead the Tub drops in for a rub-down from his personal masseuse, Erika.

Next stop Wembley, with his close friend the Duchess of Kent, to present the FA Cup to the captain of Moneybags United.

The glamour doesn't end there, as it's off to Cardiff by helicopter to judge the final of 'Ms Sheep Wales '94'.

After dinner with the winning sheep, where else but Stringfellows, for Joan Collins' 73rd birthday bash. Unfortunately the evening ends on a sad note as the Tub of Lard is mistaken for a vol-au-vent and consumed by Britain's best-loved agony columnist, Clare Rayner.

WORM CHEATS ALL WASHED UP

Authorities are clamping down on cheating at the All-British Worm charming Championships, in which contestants have fifteen minutes to charm as many worms as possible from a 4ft by 3ft patch of earth.

Competitors use a number of aids, including bagpipes, clog dancing, best bitter and champagne. Surprised no one's tried a fork.

To prevent cheating, the practice of pouring Fairy Liquid on to the worms' heads is now regarded as physical cruelty and is outlawed. However, playing non-stop Sacha Distel tapes, as one man did, is apparently perfectly permissible. So mental cruelty's obviously okay.

SCORE FOR TEAM THEN SCORE WITH MY MISSUS

Hemet football coach Randy Brown has been on trial together with his wife in California, after offering her as an incentive to his under-age team.

A good pass was rewarded with a kiss, a vital tackle was rewarded with oral sex, and every goal was rewarded with full sex. Just as well they don't have penalty shoot-outs in American Football.

Several players have now been transferred to the Hemet team, the most recent for $40 000. He said that was all he could afford.

As a result of Mr Brown's training methods, Hemet shot from being no-hopers to California Bowl finalists. If only Mrs Graham Taylor had volunteered her services for England's World Cup qualifying games – or perhaps she did.

Following the guilty verdict, Mrs Brown's now gone down for five years. So no change there.

George Best admits that the days when the world's most beautiful women flocked to his side are drawing to a close.

COPS LOSE AT SOCCER... SO THEY NICK THE REF

The Malawi Northern Region Police soccer team, who were trailing 8-3 in a league match, tried to arrest the referee but actually failed to do so because he ran off into the crowd.

What they did manage, though, was to close down the opposition attack by detaining their centre forward and torturing him for six hours. A technique also adopted recently by Arsenal.

A police spokesman said, 'The striker was not tortured, he was just made to sing the Police Federation Marching Song and serve tea to the Chief Inspector.' It would probably have been preferable to be tortured.

BURGLARS 6 SOCCER MAN 0

Soccer commentator Charles Harrison of Metro Radio, Tyne and Wear, suffered repeated burglaries every time he was out commentating on a Sunderland away match.

Harrison said the burglaries seriously affected his work: 'I was becoming more concerned about what was happening off the field rather than on it.' A not uncommon problem if you're following Sunderland.

VEGAN SPOON RACE

THE VEGAN SOCIETY say they want to ban egg-and-spoon races because they are cruel to hens.

A fair point, as hens always come last – they just can't hold the spoon without falling over.

Vegans won't eat honey because it's cruel to bees. They won't drink milk because it's cruel to cows, and they'll only wear plastic shoes. That's pretty cruel to whoever has to wash their socks.

Among the clamour of Vegan voices condemning egg and spoon races as cruel to eggs is Uri Geller, which is pretty rich given his track record with spoons.

Claims that extra-hot curry was used to fire up this year's Grand National winner are confirmed by the jockey who came second.

SPORT

KEr LICKs T_EM TO SEE Ir THEY'VE BEEN ON ALE

A dope scandal has rocked the world of snail racing after it was discovered that feeding alcohol to snails slows them down.

Now sixty-year-old match referee Simon Preston has to lick each entrant to check if they're clean. He's volunteered to do the same job at next month's women's breaststroke championships.

One monster ten-inch snail called Hector, from Woolacombe Bay in Devon, actually *likes* lager. Which means that he's useless at racing, but has now entered a darts tournament.

Snail racing is apparently big business nowadays. Ex-Grand National jockey Ron Hyett quit horse racing after twenty-three years to set up a snail farm. He's now working on a saddle that's small enough.

Curiously, snail-breeding can be problematic, as all snails have both male and female features. So presumably they both complain they've got a headache and both leave their socks on throughout.

I bet he drinks Carling Black Label!

WHY PAUL'S PIGEONS ARE REALLY FLYING HIGH

PIGEON-RACER Paul Osborne has admitted to feeding his birds cannabis, after which they won twelve first places, often arriving two hours ahead of the rest.

They probably thought they were greyhounds.

Since they've been taking cannabis, the pigeons have gained stamina and speed, although they have started listening to Jefferson Airplane and reading *The Hobbit*.

Race organisers said any pigeons found consuming drugs would be banned, just as soon as they'd worked out a way of taking a urine sample. Apparently getting a pigeon to hit a test-tube from 100 ft is a messy business.

Osborne was in court on charges of growing cannabis, but was let off the hook after the jury accepted his story that it was purely for the benefit of the birds. A large crate of racing pigeons was yesterday delivered to the home of Mr Keith Richards.

Nike sole survivors hit the beaches

A SLICK of 45 000 Nike training shoes has appeared on the Californian coast, after being washed overboard from a Korean freighter in 1990.

Californians described it as a major disaster – the shoes are almost five years out of fashion.

Enterprising beachcombers are now collecting and selling the shoes. 'I got my pair for $20,' said one local. 'That's about a quarter of the price I would have paid in a store.' And if he'd bought them in a store they wouldn't have had a couple of starfish in them either. Or seaweed for laces.

Ecologists are not so happy at the prospect of all those rubber shoes fouling the coastline. The US coastguards now plan to disperse them with four tons of odour eaters.

CUBANS SET GAMES RECORD

In one week, a record thirty-four Cuban athletes have defected from the Central American Games.

Even the team's security man has gone missing. He was hired from the well-known Cuban firm Gruppo Quatro.

Two of the defectors were the gold and silver medal-winners in the 4000-metre cycle race, as they brushed past the finishing tape, past the podium, past the long-jump pit, the security guards, the exit doors, the border and off into the sunset.

People in Britain are astonished that Fidel Castro's left-wing regime has allowed Cuban's champion high-jumper to keep only 30 per cent of his prize of £25 000 and a Mercedes. Still, under the last Labour government here, he'd have been allowed to keep just 2 per cent. That's five hundred quid and the fluffy dice.

It's not just athletes who are defecting – one Cuban photographer who got into the USA advised his fellow countrymen to do as he did and bring with them examples of their work over the last ten years. Let's hope no mortuary attendants try to defect.

ODD ONE OUT

JOHN MAJOR

DR DOOLITTLE

PERCY EDWARDS

NORMAN LAMONT

> *Dr Doolittle is next door to Mr Do-little on the top there. It's something to do with talking to animals.*

> *So, do you want to pick one out?*

> *Why? Why can't we just all be friends? Why do you have to isolate people like this?*

> *Is it John Major?*

> *I think it's Norman Lamont.*

The odd one out *is* John Major, as the others are all capable of impersonating animals. John Major has nevertheless been described as 'a beast in bed', on account of his thin lips. Expert physiognomist Lailan Young explained, 'The thinner the lips are, the more enthusiastic the lover.' Good news for Norma, bad news for Jerry Hall.

Norman Lamont is a keen ornithologist and can apparently impersonate an owl. He's certainly got the eyebrows for it.

Dr Doolittle famously used to talk with the animals, one being a remarkable two-headed creature which the doctor brought back to England and which later became leader of the Liberal Democrats.

Percy Edwards used to receive parcels of birdseed from listeners whenever he did his bird impersonations, was sent numerous packets of dog biscuits whenever he did his dog impressions, and lived to regret the one time he impersonated a dung beetle.

> *I said it was John Major.*

> *Yes, but you were overruled by your captain unfortunately.*

> *Overruled? Since when have I had the power to overrule anybody? I overrule you, then. Go on, piss off out of it – we could get Noel Edmonds doing this.*

NEWS JUST IN

Deng Xiao Ping makes a guest appearance in the Chinese version of *Baywatch*.

Following the army clamp-down on fraternisation between soldiers of the same sex, the Irish Guards hit upon an ingenious solution.

A new scandal rocks the world of cricket, as Mike Atherton is photographed attempting to rub soap on the ball.

A recently discovered archive photo suggests that Sherlock Holmes' drug problem was worse than originally suspected.

... and the first meeting is held of the Sellafield Skydiving Club.

And finally …

CHRISTMAS CAPTION COMPETITION

I suppose a Santa sandwich is out of the question.

I always end up with men that only come once a year …

'I thought you were a made-up fictional character,' says Santa.

… yeah, but they do fill your stockings.

… and when they do, it's down the chimney …